BADMINTON

PLAY THE GAME

BADMINTON

PAT DAVIS

BLANDFORD

First published in Great Britain in 1988
This revised edition published in 1993 by
Blandford, Wellington House, 125 Strand,
London WC2R 0BB.
A Cassell Imprint

Reprinted 1994, 1995, 1996

Designed by Anita Ruddell
Illustrations by Jerry Malone

Text set in Helvetica
by Hourds Typographica, Stafford, England
Printed and bound in Great Britain
by The Bath Press, Avon

British Library Cataloguing in Publication Data

Davis, Pat, *1915-*
   Play the game: badminton
   1. Badminton. Manual
   I. Title
     796.34'5

ISBN 0 7137 2415 3

Acknowledgments

The author and publishers would like to
thank Colorsport for supplying the
photographs used in this book.

**Frontispiece: Huang Hua closes on the
net for a backhand which, with power and
timing, she can send to the back of the
court or drop delicately over the net.**

CONTENTS

FOREWORD

I am delighted to have been asked to prepare a foreword for this exciting new publication, and am pleased to give it my full support as President of the English Schools Badminton Association.

Badminton is smashing – those of us who have been around long enough need no convincing of that fact – and who are we to hog the finest of games? No, we like to share our enjoyment with *all* would-be wielders of a badminton racket.

In Ward Lock's new *Play the Game* series, badminton has been given an expert treatment by Pat Davis, the doyen of the badminton writing fraternity. A potted history of the game provides enough background to show that England was the motivator for this exciting and now worldwide game of badminton. (The Badminton Association of England celebrates its century in 1993.) This explanation of the origins of the game is followed by detailed information on all aspects of how to play the game. For the beginner, the descriptions are easy to understand, practical and not clouded with theory. The numerous illustrations are good and clear, and they reinforce all the descriptive points, from equipment to techniques. Once the beginner has had the appetite whetted in the opening sections of the book, and can appreciate the basics, then the finer techniques are presented to savour and ponder.

I wish all readers of this fine new book success in developing the skills which bring such personal enjoyment and satisfaction to all badminton players worldwide. They will need good speed and stamina in order to attain these, but this book explains how to get fit for badminton as well as how to play it. A final word: remember, as this book makes patently clear – for success, *keep it simple*.

Thomas A. Bowker
President of the English Schools Badminton Association

HISTORY &
DEVELOPMENT OF
BADMINTON

Badminton is a fascinating game! One moment you are striking the shuttle with all your strength, the next you are stroking it delicately with millimetre-upward accuracy. At top level, it is the most demanding of racket games, calling for a fencer's speed of reflex and a gymnast's agility. And yet a beginner can have a fun game the first time he plays.

Its equipment of 100gm ($3\frac{1}{2}$oz) racket and 5gm ($\frac{1}{6}$oz). shuttlecock (which for all its frailty can achieve 160km/h (100mph) off the racket) are marvels of modern precision engineering and aerodynamics. And being so light they enable you to use very satisfying deception and to play the game to a ripe old age. I should know! After over fifty years' play, I still enjoy a game as much as ever.

Badminton's origins add a touch of glamour to the game. Its gentle forerunner, battledore and shuttlecock, in which the aim was to keep a rally going, not to end it, was played in Ancient Greece and early Far Eastern civilizations (who sometimes used feet rather than rackets!). Medieval woodcuts show it being played with primitive, home-made rackets and shuttles. Nineteenth-century illustrations depict it as a languid game for the elegant and wealthy. And indeed it was played by the children of the Duke of Beaufort at his Gloucestershire mansion, Badminton House. If you visit it today you will be shown the crude battledore and big shuttles they used. On one of them is a remarkable inscription 'Kept up with Geraldine Somerset on Saturday 12th January to *2117*. Henrietta Somerset'. Incredible concentration for a young girl. Try it for yourself!

From those children's games it is thought that badminton was born. Army officers on leave from India with nothing better to do on a rainy day picked up the children's toys and played the first *competitive* game. A frequent visitor to Badminton House, John Lorraine Baldwin, may have devised the first crude laws as he had done for various card games. The first official rules were made in Poona, India, in 1877.

It was not until 1893 that the Badminton Association was formed with just fourteen clubs. They realized that the rules and court sizes varying in length from 13·4–18m

(44–60ft) as well as shuttle speeds, ranging from cab-horse slow to rocket fast, must be standardized. By 1914 there were 467 clubs, in 1923, 550 clubs and by 1934 there were 1000 clubs. Today there are 5,500 affiliated clubs. And double that number of unaffiliated clubs who enjoy the benefits of a well-organized game but are loath to pay the small fees. Apart from these there are thousands of people playing individually at sports centres.

In 1934, the Badminton Association relinquished world-wide control of the fast growing game to the International Badminton Federation (IBF). It has continued, however, as the Badminton Association of England (BA of E), to do an excellent job in England of popularizing and improving the game at all levels from club to international. The All-England Championships, which have become badminton's Wimbledon and, unofficially, World Championships, started in 1899. After the IBF official World Championships, they are still the most prestigious and best organized championships in the world. Go to see them and watch the world's top players in thrilling action on Wembley Arena's seven fine courts. It's an unforgettable occasion!

On a lower level, in 1928/29, came the Inter-County Championships, the backbone of English badminton. Today, every county in England takes part; over a hundred I, II and III teams are put on court. In their own right, County Associations have done much to further the game in their own areas by forming leagues and running a wide range of tournaments which can be enjoyed by players of varied levels of skill. Don't miss out on these: they are great fun and a fine means of improving your play.

When life settled back to normal after World War II, the BA of E took another big step forward when they formed a Coaching Committee who organized courses for players, and for very necessary would-be coaches. Today, in addition to top flight coaches such as Jake Downey, Paul Whetnall and Roger Mills there are many hundreds of other trained coaches eager to help players at all levels in specially organized courses.

This coaching led to the emergence at an early age of such brilliant international players as Steve Baddeley, Darren Hall, Steve Butler, Andy Goode, Anders Nielsen, Gillian Clark and Gillian Gower.

Although one of the strongest sides in Europe, England have not yet won major world individual or team championships. The meteoric rise first of Malaysia, then Indonesia, and now China has put paid to that.

The BA of E has done a tremendous job for English badminton. Similar excellent organizations are at work, largely voluntarily, in Wales, Ireland and Scotland.

The essential foundation of the game, the English Schools Badminton Association, must not be forgotten. This body, under the dedicated direction of Eric Brown and other volunteers, not only nurtures budding internationals but also teaches the game to

One of the logos used by the English Schools Badminton Association.

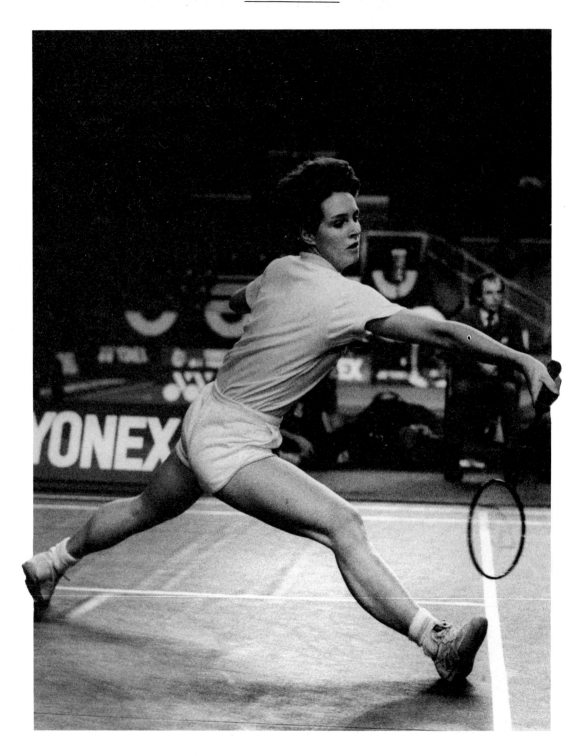

tens of thousands of less brilliant youngsters to give them interest, exercise and fun for years to come.

Lastly, but not least, the International Badminton Federation. Today it controls the ever spreading game in currently over sixty countries from the Falklands to Kuwait, from Malaysia to America, from Malta to Mozambique. It organizes major events such as the individual World Championships as well as the two team Championship events, the Thomas Cup (men) and the Uber Cup (ladies), both named after famous English players. There is also a Grand Prix tournament, the Seiko, which incorporates some fifteen other major tournaments played around the world. In this wide international scene names to remember are Morten Frost and Kirsten Larsen (Denmark); the five Sidek brothers (Malaysia); Han Aiping, Li Lingwei, Zhao Jianhua, Li Yongbo, Yang Yang (China); Ivana Lie, Liem Swie King, Hartono (Indonesia); Sumiko Kitada (Japan); Christine Magnusson and Maria Bengtsson (Sweden); Joo Bong Park and Yun Ja Kim (South Korea) . . . and dozens more first class players.

All of which goes to show that badminton has an exciting international flavour. However,for the moment all that concerns you is that almost immediately you will be able to play a simple game and let off steam, have fun and get plenty of exercise. In this country badminton is played indoors, but in some Asian countries where there are very still evenings, outdoors. (Don't try outdoors here unless you want the laugh of the century as you vainly try to hit a shuttle that veers disconcertingly away from your racket at the slightest breath of wind). It is therefore an ideal winter game that laughs at rain and fog, darkness and snow. But some enthusiasts do play through the summer as well. That's how badminton grabs you!

Have a good game, and keep on practising and learning. Above all *enjoy* it. Badminton is fun. I know!

England international Helen Troke reaches the shuttle in one swift movement from mid-court. Once the shot has been made she will regain her central position in preparation for the next return.

EQUIPMENT & TERMINOLOGY

Before starting to learn how to play badminton, it is important to familiarize yourself with the equipment needed, and the terminology you will come across as you get to grips with the game.

EQUIPMENT

Avoid the twin evils of paying too little or too much for your equipment. But do buy the best you can afford. Good equipment does not necessarily make a good player but it certainly helps.

Rackets

Obviously your racket is of prime importance. Choose it thoughtfully. A reasonable racket can be bought for £20, a perfectly adequate one for £40. The £60–90 price range is for the fanatic. Famous names count: Carlton, Slazenger, RSL, Yonex . . .

Handle Check that this is just the right and therefore comfortable size for you. The range of sizes from 8·6–9·2cm ($3\frac{3}{8}$–$3\frac{5}{8}$in) is seemingly small but choose one that feels neither too small so that you cannot hold it effectively, or too big so that you hold it too tightly. Make sure it has a grip on it that lives up to its name even when your hands are

damp. Leather is best; towelling tends to become matted.

Shaft The material varies with price, ranging from tempered steel to graphite, graphite and fibreglass, graphite and boron, and recently graphite and ceramic fibre. Do not be bewildered by this list – steel will do, graphite, with additives, gives ever greater durability and lightness. 100gm ($3\frac{1}{2}$oz) is the right weight.

Whichever you choose it should have whip, i.e. bend slightly. To test this, hold the racket horizontally by the top of the head with one hand and at the end of the handle with the other. Press upwards *gently* (no snapped shafts in the shop, please!) and the shaft should flex slightly.

Frame This again may be graphite and its additives, or aluminium. Avoid all-steel, for they tend to be cumbersome and ill-balanced. It should be rigid, and 'channelled' so that the strings are not scraped if you scoop up a shuttle from the floor. To prevent the strings rubbing against the metal frame and fraying, see that the holes are lined with soft plastic protectors, i.e. grommets.

T-piece The head and shaft, if of graphite, etc. are moulded in one piece. If metal, they

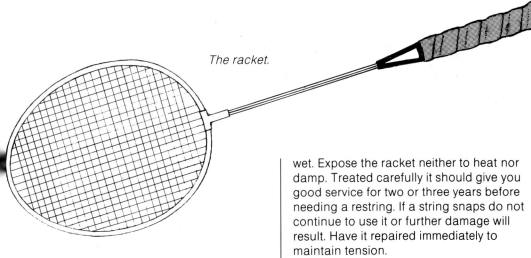

The racket.

are joined by a T-piece. This join is known, reasonably, as the throat. In a very few models it may be 'open', to save weight.

Strings   Most important of all, since they provide the impetus to enable you to hit a shuttle hard and fast, are the strings. Natural gut is the best. It has more resilience than synthetic gut – and is correspondingly more expensive. The best such gut is clear and thin. The best synthetic guts are either oil-filled or multi-minuscule (filled with microscopic fibres).

Whichever you choose its tensioning is vitally important. If it is too tight, especially with synthetic guts, it is difficult to control or 'feel' the shuttle in delicate strokes; if too slack, it is difficult to hit hard. Normally strings should be tensioned at about 5·9kg (13lb).

Two basic tension tests are these. Flick your fingernail lightly across the strings – they should give a crisp 'ping'. And if you hold your racket head with the thumbs on either side of the frame and press the stringing with them it should give – *very* slightly.

Care   To get the best out of your carefully chosen racket, take care of it. Never throw or bounce it on the floor in bad temper. Use a head-cover to ensure the strings do not get

wet. Expose the racket neither to heat nor damp. Treated carefully it should give you good service for two or three years before needing a restring. If a string snaps do not continue to use it or further damage will result. Have it repaired immediately to maintain tension.

Shuttles

Badminton's 'ball' is the fragile and aerodynamically efficient shuttlecock. It weighs in at an average 4·8gm (80 grains) i.e. roughly 6 to an ounce!

Feathered and synthetic   There are two types: the original feathered, and the comparatively recently-invented substitute, the synthetic. Both have a domed base of cork or polyurethane containing the tiny lead weight without which the shuttle would be too light to fly the necessary distances. To this is attached the 'skirt', in one case of sixteen feathers, in the other, of a synthetic material.

Top players play only with feathered shuttles. Synthetic shuttles are perfectly acceptable for beginners and most club players. 'Gold' coloured synthetics are a good choice in halls with light backgrounds. And 'cold' synthetics last longer in cold weather. Prices (Synthetic £4 to £9 per dozen; feathered £7 to £12 per dozen) and durability vary widely. Considerable savings can be made by dealing with the numerous mail order firms who advertise regularly in the BA of E official magazine, *Badminton*.

Feathered shuttles were once far more expensive than synthetic; today, some

The feathered shuttlecock.

The synthetic shuttlecock.

correct speed needed in your hall. Some shuttles, generally synthetic, are colour-graded 'slow', 'medium' and 'fast'. Virtually all feathered shuttles are numerically graded from 73–85. These figures indicate the weight – in grains (a grain = 0·065g) – and therefore the speed. A 73 will travel some 10–15cm (4–6in) less distance than a 74, and so on, with 85s being the fastest.

The speed you should use depends on the size and temperature of the hall you play in – in other words, on the air-resistance. In a small, heated, one-court hall you might use a 75, while if it was unheated, a 78; in cavernous, modern sports centres you might need an 82.

Once you can hit effectively, find out for yourself the correct speed by the following test. Holding the shuttle *directly over the base-line* hit it hard, underhand, straight, at an upward angle of 45°. If it is the correct speed, it will drop not less than 0·53m (1ft 9in) (too fast) and not more than 1·0m (3ft 3in) (too slow) short of the other back boundary line.

Care A shuttle's life, especially when mis-hit, is all too short – and expensive. So treat them with loving care!
1. *Never* hit them on the half-volley.
2. *Don't* crush or bang their container.
3. *Never* store feathered shuttles in heat.
4. *Always* smooth ruffled plumes between thumb and forefinger.
5. *Play* with the correct speed.

Shoes

What you wear on your feet is far more important than what you wear on your body. Shoes are the foundation of all-important speed. They should be as light and *flexible* as is possible commensurate with having some interior cushioning. A soft but rough or ridged sole (not black) is essential for the grip needed for stopping, starting and turning. Nylon and suede are often used in

brands are no more or even less expensive than synthetic ones. Make sure, however, if you opt for them, that the feathers are strong *goose* feathers, not the weaker *duck* feathers. Base your choice on price, tested durability, and the type used by your friends or club. It is not advisable to switch from one type to the other. Here again, great names count: RSL, DSS, Carlton, Yonex.

Correct speed Whichever shuttles you choose make sure they are tested for the

Badminton clothing.

the uppers. The lacing should be grommeted and from toe to instep, and the tongue lightly padded. A padded, heel tab support may mitigate against Achilles tendon trouble. Strong toe-guard and toe-cap are essential to prevent wear by dragging the foot.

Heavy, hard soled trainers are the last thing you should wear if speed and balance are your aim. Dirty shoes betoken a sloppy player. So keep them clean – and fresh!

Clothing

This is largely a matter of personal preference. Many very attractive outfits are available. Men wear shorts, shirt and sweater; ladies, the same, but with the alternatives of skirt, dress or cardigan. The colour should be predominantly white and of modern fashion; using colour sparingly but effectively is permissible. White socks too of course.

Garments should be short, of absorbent and easily washed material, and never so tight or long as to restrict movement. Off-court a track-suit is a useful adjunct that will keep you warm after a hard game and so help prevent pulled muscles. Never play in one except perhaps in the knock-up; it looks sloppy and hampers easy action. Give thought to your clothes. 'Whites' are not

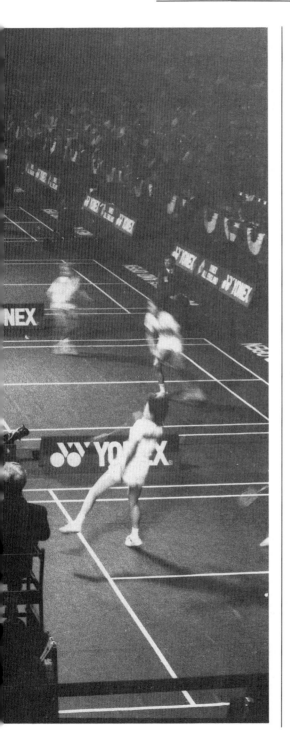

essential for informal school or sports centre knockabouts. But whatever you wear, if you look smart and attractive you will look *and feel* like a player.

Off-court bag

Once you play in matches or tournaments, an off-court bag can be a wise provision. As play must be continuous, it should cater for all emergencies: an extra racket of the same weight and tension as that generally used, safety pins, sweat-bands, towel, a salted glucose drink, talc for sweaty hands, spectacles demisting agent (assuming you wear them, that is!), elastoplasts, hair bandeau – and a copy of the Laws for a friendly settlement of any disputes.

The court

The accompanying diagrams speak louder than words in regard to names and distances. Obviously, to be able to communicate, you must know the former and it is helpful and advisable to know the latter.

An ideal court will have a clear height of 9·1m (30ft), be marked out with lines 3·8cm (1½in) wide and be 1·52m (5ft) at least from a back wall and 0·9m (3ft) from a neighbouring court. For good sighting of the shuttle, daylight should be without glare; artificial light, above the posts, without dazzle. Background walls should be a matt dull green. The floor should be smooth but not slippery. Posts are set *on* the outside lines so as to keep the net taut: 1·54m (5ft 1in) near the post and 1·52m (5ft) in the centre. These measurements are taken from the floor to the top of the net.

Sadly very few courts live up to these ideals. But badminton is still played – and enjoyed – in much more difficult 'rabbit-

The early rounds in the All England Championship, Wembley arena.

The doubles court.

The singles court.

*Measurements include line widths

---

hutch' conditions where a strong backswing results in a snapped racket, and the luckless shuttle has to traverse a maze of low beams, lights and heaters in glare or gloom!

Where to play

Schools and clubs obviously have their own courts. As the latter are chary of accepting complete beginners, there are two options:

1 Book a court, with a friend, at your local sports centre.

2 Join an Adult Study Centre evening class where you will also get tuition. If still in doubt ask at your local newspaper office or local sports outfitters shop.

TERMINOLOGY

Angled drive serve   The idea of all serves is to try and 'con' your opponent. The angled drive serve is a 'con' of a 'con' – the drive. For the angled drive serve you stand as far to the right of the service court as you can within the laws, and then kid your opponent into thinking you are going to serve a low serve but then make it a drive. Standing to the right of the service court will give you that extra width to play across court with.

Attacking clear   An advanced overhead attacking stroke, hit low and fast to the back line of your opponent's court.

Backhand low serve   The same as the low serve, but played on the backhand. The high or very high serve are never played on the backhand, and the drive serve only infrequently.

Bird   Another name for the shuttlecock.

Danish wipe   (also known as Swedish swish). A cross between a drive and a lob.

Defensive clear   The more commonly-used defensive version of the attacking clear. It is an overhead stroke hitting the shuttle high from one baseline to the other.

Drive serve   This is another 'disguised serve'. It appears to be a standard low serve but at the last moment the racket head is speeded up and the serve driven to a part of the opposing court where you know your opponent is at his weakest.

Flick serve   To all intents and purposes this serve looks like a low serve to your opponent, but at the very last minute you uncock your wrist and slightly loft the shuttle, which will go towards the back of the court and, hopefully, catch your opponent unaware.

Forehand smash   An attacking stroke. The object is to hit the shuttle down as fast and as steeply over the net as possible. There is also a backhand version.

High serve   A serve played with such loft that it forces your opponent to the back of the court. It blunts his smash, and opens up the front of the court.

Let   When a point has to be replayed a 'let' is called.

Lob   A defensive forehand or backhand stroke, played underhand and used to return a shuttle which is well below tape-level, in the forecourt, high to the baseline.

Low serve   A delicate serve that starts to dip before crossing the tape. It is the 'bread and butter' serve and if played accurately forces a 'lift' because the receiver cannot play down on to the shuttle.

Net shots   A variety of shots played *from* near the net and often very near *to* the net.

Overhead drop shot   A deceptive shot, disguised as a smash, but just gently dropped over the net. If it is not a winning shot it will have drawn your opponent near to the net. Used more in singles than doubles.

Rush   A fast movement forward by the receiver to dab the shuttle aggressively down for a winner.

Swedish swish   See Danish wipe.

Tape   The white tape at the top of the net.

Very high serve   Similar to a high serve, but hit as high as your strength, and the roof, allow, to make timing difficult for your opponent.

THE GAME –
A GUIDE

THE · RULES · OF ·
BADMINTON

Badminton can be played as singles or doubles, either men's, women's or mixed. It is a volleying game and the shuttlecock must not hit the ground during a rally or the rally is lost.

Most matches consist of the best-of-three games. A game is won by the first player or pair to reach 15 points (11 in ladies' singles).

Like squash, in badminton it is only the server who can win points. If the non-server wins the rally then he becomes the server and has the chance to score points thereafter. (Singles).

Commencing a game and serving

The players toss a coin or spin a racket to decide who shall serve first. Serving is done diagonally and the first serve is from the right-hand service court. The server alternates between the right and left service courts until the serve is lost. When the new· server takes his first serve, it is always from the service court that he is then in. When a pair regains the serve from its opponents, the first serve is always from the right-hand service court.

In doubles play, each side has two 'chances' with the serve. If they lose the rally on the first serve they do not pass the service to the opposing side, but instead the second member of the team serves. If they lose the rally on **his** serve though, they **do** lose the serve. At the start of a doubles game however, the initial pairing is allowed **only** one service chance.

In doubles, it is the serving pair who alternate between service courts, not the receiving pair. They stay put . . . in *singles* play, both players change sides for every new service: if they didn't, the server would have an easy job . . . there would be nobody in the receiving half of the court! If the server's score is an odd number, 1, 3, 5, etc., then service commences in, and to, the left service court. If it is even, 2, 4, 6, etc., it starts in, and to, the right service court.

The server must stand entirely within the service court and with part of **both** feet on the ground. The shuttle must be hit underarm and the racket must make contact with it below the server's waist. The receiving player must be in the court diagonally opposite and must also have part of both feet on the ground. Once the serve has been returned, players may move around at random. In doubles play, the players do **not** have to play the shuttle in sequence, as in table tennis. Badminton is a very much more flexible game in this respect.

Opening positions:
beginning a game of doubles

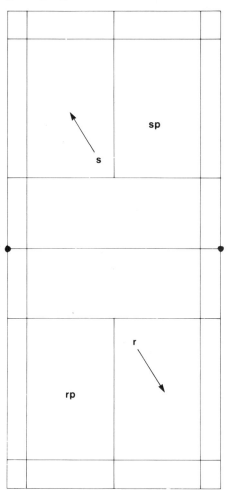

s = server
sp = server's partner
r = receiver
rp = receiver's partner
- - - - = movement.

Setting

Once the scores reach 13-all in all disciplines (except ladies singles), the match can be set to 5. This means the first player (or team) who reached 13, after it became 13-all, can either carry on to 15 as if nothing had happened or opt to play a further 5 points. In this case the scores are set at 0-0 and play commences until one player (team) reaches 5. If the score is then say 5-3, a score of 18-16 is registered, not 5-3.

The same setting option is open once the scores reach 14-all, but this time the game can be only set to 3.

In ladies' singles setting is to 3 at 9-all or to 2 at 10-all.

Setting is not allowed in handicap games.

Changing ends

Ends are changed at the completion of each game, and if the match goes to a deciding game ends are changed when one player or pair reaches 8. In ladies' singles the change is made at 6.

The rally

The rally continues until one player makes a fault. There are a number of ways he can do this. The most common by far are:
(a) Missing the shuttle completely
(b) Failing to hit it over the net
(c) Hitting it into the net
(d) Hitting it outside the court boundary lines, either in service or in play
(e) touching the net either with his body or racket while the shuttle is 'in play'
(f) Hitting the shuttle twice in succession with two strokes.
Other much less common faults are dealt with in the **Rules Clinic.**

Scoring

Some people believe scoring in badminton to be difficult; well, it's actually not!

BADMINTON

If you remember the following basic points, scoring is easy:

(a) When the serving side win a rally, they add a point to their score; when they lose a rally, they lose one player's serve

(b) When the receiving side win a rally, they do not get a point but they have taken one of their opponents' serves away; when they lose a rally their opponents gain a point. Practise scoring until it's as natural as breathing. Anyone who can't score tends to look a bit of a clot.

One player should be elected to call the score aloud at the end of each rally.

The score starts at 0-0, called 'love-all'. The serving side's score is called first. If they win the rally and lead 1-0, that is the score called. If they lose the next rally it is then the turn of the second player to serve. The score is called '1-0 second server', '2-0 second server', and so on.

When a rally is lost and service passes to the other side, the score is called as 0-1 (assuming that was the score at the time the service passed over!). When it passes to the second server of that side it is '0-1 second server'. Always put the serving side's score first.

Right, you've learnt the rules, and hopefully you now understand scoring and setting. If you don't, then read them again. When you get on court, you should, at the earliest opportunity, take upon yourself the task of scoring. That is the best way to learn. You will make mistakes but, let's face it, it is really the only way to learn properly.

RULES
CLINIC

Can I do an overhead Boris Becker serve at badminton?

No. This would be a fault for two reasons: (a) at impact part or all of the shuttle would be well above the top of the hip-bone and (b) the racket head would also be clearly above the hand holding it. Both heinous badminton crimes.

When serving, can I pretend to hit the shuttle one way – then hit it the other?

Yes, provided that the racket is in *continuous* motion throughout. With the same proviso, you can deceptively speed up or slow down the movement of the racket.

If the shuttle when served strikes the net-cord, can I claim a 'let' or replay as in tennis?

No, there are no 'lets' for this in badminton, so the shuttle should be played. It is, however, a fault if the shuttle actually stays on the tape, or is caught in the net on the receiver's side – but it's a million-to-one chance! During a rally, such an occurrence would be a 'let'.

You say 'Don't hurry when serving or taking up a receiving stance'. How long am I allowed?

There must be no *undue* delay. Say seven seconds?

If I anticipate my opponent's serve may I move to intercept it before he actually hits the shuttle?

No, it is a fault to move before the shuttle is struck.

What happens if a server serves before I'm ready?

Provided you make no attempt to play it you can claim a let.

What happens if I hit the shuttle over the net on the frame or shaft?

Provided it is one clean hit, it is quite legal. It is, however, a fault if you 'sling' the shuttle, i.e. hit the shuttle in a curving trajectory after 'holding' it momentarily on your racket (probably between frame and strings). You must declare such a fault yourself.

If I see an opponent is going to kill a shot at the net may I protect my face with my racket?

Yes, provided you do not baulk or distract him by waving the racket about.

What happens if I miss the shuttle altogether or just touch it when serving?

The shuttle has not crossed the net so it is a fault.

Service faults

What an horrific picture!
Four foul serves in one!
Can you spot them?

Does it matter if I hit the net in my follow through?

It is a fault. So too, if during play, you touch the net in any way, put a foot under it, slide bodily under it, or let your racket fly over it. You have invaded your opponent's court.

If a shuttle hits only the outside edge of a line is it 'in' or 'out'?

The lines bounding a court are 'in', no matter how little of them is touched. Conversely, if, when serving or receiving, you stand, even fractionally, on a line, your foot is *outside* the court: a fault.

Can I jump to play a shot?

By all means, except when you are serving or waiting to receive. Then you must have part of each foot in contact with the floor in the service court opposite your opponent. Conversely you may play a shot when lying on the floor; some players can do it.

Can I hit a shuttle before it is on my side of the net?

No. To do so is a fault because, if left, your opponent's shot might have been too tight to the net for you to return. You may however follow through over the net provided you have first struck the shuttle on your side.

If I hit the shuttle or am hit by it when I'm standing outside the line, may I still claim the shuttle is 'out'?

No, whether you are 'in' or 'out' of the court and are hit by the shuttle, it is a fault.

Do we play on if the shuttle just grazes my hair, my racket or my clothing before my partner hits the shuttle?

You must declare a 'touch' even though, as a fault, it loses you the rally.

What do we do if a shuttle touches a roof beam or girder?

Clubs have their own rules on this. Generally, hitting a girder results in a 'let'. Hitting the roof itself is a fault as this could be done deliberately.

May I stop in a game or between games to get my wind back or to get advice from my coach?

No. Play must be continuous.

What is the position if the shuttle is badly damaged in mid-rally?

Play continues unless 'skirt' and base part company completely, when a 'let' would be played.

Taking the shuttle too early.

Are these all the Laws?

All you need to start with. The full Laws can be bought very cheaply at sports outfitters or obtained from the Badminton Association of England, whose address appears on page 77.

TECHNIQUE

BODY · TALK

Badminton is a very physical game demanding quick movement and hard hitting with only a matter of seconds between long rallies. It is therefore important to realize that in every stroke several parts of the body must synchronize to produce an effective shot.

All power strokes are a form of throwing. And by uncocking your wrist just before impact (which is generally just in front of the body) the racket-head is moving at its fastest in what we call the 'zip' or 'zing' area (45·7cm (18in) either side of impact). Perfect timing results.

Eye

The old maxim 'keep your eye on the shuttle' is still a valid one. Pick up its line of flight immediately it leaves your opponent's racket,

Perfect body control – everything synchronized for an ideal stroke: balanced feet; knees bent; body leaning into stroke; elbow bent; correct grip; early and full backswing; eyes on the shuttle.

Stockport
Library,Advice _Information Service
You should retain this receipt.

Borrowed Items 05/11/2015 13:53
XXXXXXXXXX1629

Item Title   Due Date

* Clayshooting : a   26/11/20
complete guide to skeet,
trap and sporting
shooting

Badminton   26/11/2015
Soccer   17/11/2015

*Indicates items borrowed today
Thankyou for using this service
www.stockport.gov.uk/libraries
Tel 0161 217 6009

watch the shuttle onto the very strings of your own racket and you will be spared the ignominy of miss or mis-hit.

When hitting upwards, keep your head down for a fraction *after* impact. If you look up just before impact, thinking you can't miss it – you may well do so. If you look up to see where the shuttle is going, it is very likely it won't go anywhere.

Fast feet

In a game played over a 1.52m (5ft) net and with a 'ball' that is not allowed to bounce (even if it could!), it is impossible to overstate the need for speed of movement and good balance. And on a small half-court, only 6·0 × 6·7m (22 × 20ft), badminton movement is a series of short, sharp movements of no more than four or five paces. These involve good braking, quick starting, bending, stretching, turning, jumping and last second changes of direction – almost an acrobat's routine. Even if you are only fractionally slow, a split second, in meeting the shuttle, it may have fallen below tape-height. And you have lost the chance to attack!

Exercises for speed   Never be self-conscious about running – it's vital and half the fun of the game, Several things contribute to this exciting turn of speed. Obviously strong legs and ankles help to give initial and essential acceleration. Exercises, such as step-ups, squat-jumps, bunny hops, star-jumps, and skipping, both for lightness and power, will help.

Observation plays its part   Equally important as a fast start is an early start. If you move to the shuttle as soon as it is struck, you will get to it earlier than a faster runner who doesn't move until the shuttle is practically crossing the net. If you don't move early you will seldom gain the attack. To this end you must train yourself to 'read' what kind of stroke your opponent is playing almost as the shuttle leaves his racket.

Speed!
The springboard to success!

Anticipation   Although based on observation this is a rather different virtue. In other words you decide, even before the shuttle is hit, what will be your opponent's *likely* shot. After an angled drive serve to your opponent's backhand, anticipate a weak return to the net. With the shuttle behind your slow-moving opponent in rear court expect a short clear. After a smash into the body expect a cramped return lacking power. Of course this predictability cannot

The perfect position of readiness.

The latter point is of prime importance. Your feet should never be still or your body weight inertia tends to become greater, and it is therefore harder to drive into swift action. Either do a little shuffle or bounce to reduce it. Never be static!

Your racket too must be equally ready. Since you are hoping to attack, hold it at *head height* slightly forward of the body. When you are defending – that is, when you have hit the shuttle upwards – expect a hit down. So lower the racket so that it is across a likely target, your stomach. Feet are still on the move but you may prefer a rather squarer stance with the right foot slightly forward.

Actual movement   This should be light and well-balanced. Moving forward from a base-line to net you will run; moving backwards you can either run or chassé (skipping sideways, bringing one foot up to the other); the former is preferable as it is slightly faster.

Braking, acceleration and balance   Good 'braking' and recovery are equally essential. Running forward to the net generally ends in a long lunge, an action with three advantages. It reaches forward, so saving another short step, it is an excellent means of braking, and the outstretched right foot provides an effective push-off in recovery. This also applies to sideways movement. In running backwards, a final longer backward step has the advantages of the lunge. Short steps are best for initial acceleration and for instant, driving recovery.

Balance, so easily lost by a late start and stumbling movement, is also very important; good balance saves steps!

Killer instinct   Finally, yet another facet of speed. You must have in you the 'killer'

Morten Frost of Denmark – one of the finest exponents of the modern game.

be guaranteed, but you will see these results more often than not, and it's also worth remembering that most players are creatures of habit.

Position of readiness   Even for the split-second between strokes, quickly position yourself roughly centrally to avoid leaving gaping gaps. From such a thoughtfully chosen base you want a good springboard for movement. This is your 'position of readiness', the stance you immediately take up after each stroke as you regain base.

When you are attacking, you should be upright, knees slightly bent, turned slightly sideways to the net with your left foot in advance, and *on the balls of your feet.*

instinct that sends you leaping to the shuttle at the slightest possibility of a winner. And, equally, the 'never-say-die' instinct that sends you stretching, even diving to the floor, if that is going to prevent the shuttle hitting it, and the point being lost.

So use head, heart and eye as well as feet and legs to move fast. Never be slack and sluggish, unaware and unalert. Never, never just stand back and let a shuttle come to you. Always go fast to meet the shuttle early, above the tape. Then, the points will come to you.

Arm

This is the obvious generator of racket-head speed. In all power shots it must be fully bent and strongly *snapped straight* with a vigorous throwing action; never, never just pushed forward. To its speed are added those of wrist and forearm.

Forearm

Modern thinking is that the turn of the forearm is responsible for much power. When a right-hander raises his racket-head and then drops it over his shoulder into the small of his back, the forearm turns from left to right. In the actual hitting it should *pronate* strongly, i.e. turn back from right to left.

In backhand shots the opposite takes place. In the actual hitting action when the forearm turns from left to right, it *supinates*. Try it for extra power!

Wrist

This is the vital partner of the arm. Notice, with racket in hand, how it can be bent backwards ('cocked'), or forwards ('uncocked') explosively, It can also be turned to the right and to the left.

The wrist is used in every power stroke. Thereby it holds the threat of explosive power, for when it is uncocked, wrist speed is added to arm speed.

A last-second *turn* of the wrist is equally effective. This time it provides *deception,* for the shuttle which was apparently going to be played to the forehand is now turned to the backhand or vice versa. And, by keeping the uncocking of the wrist back to the last split second, 'holding', and then suddenly employing it with a slow arm action the speed *and* trajectory of the shuttle can be altered bewilderingly at the last moment.

The lunge.

Body

In all power strokes, body weight is on the back foot at the end of the preparation. It must, in the course of the stroke, be swung forwards, by turning hips and shoulders, into the line of flight of the shuttle, with the body square to the net at impact.

This thrusting of almost total bodyweight into the stroke can add considerable power. So never be afraid to bend the body backwards and turn the shoulders into a side-on position. From that position, the body weight should be spiralled upwards into overhead strokes.

For control and balance, rather than power, the same is done, much more gently, even in low serve and net-shot. In the former, the body-turn on its own is nearly enough to hit the shuttle the short distance needed. In the lob, a little more body swing is needed. In backhand drives and Danish wipes the body turn should be strongly added to the flinging of the racket.

Killer instinct!

STROKE · TECHNIQUES

The grip

Get the grip right and you're likely to get most of your strokes right. Get it wrong and . . .

There are two simple ways of obtaining the correct grip. In the first get someone to hold your racket by the head and extend the handle towards you sideways on and horizontally. Then, simply shake hands with it . . . after all it's going to be your best friend, isn't it?

In the second way, simply place your racket flat on the ground, then pick it up, sideways on, as if it were an axe.

In each case you should be able to notice the four following points:

1 The V between your thumb and forefinger is in line with the shaft.

2 Your fingers are slightly spaced apart, especially the forefinger from the second finger.

3 The butt end of the racket nestles just within the palm of your hand to give you maximum reach and leverage.

4 If you turn your hand to the right, palm upwards, and open it, you will see that the racket lies across the base of your *fingers*, rather than your palm. This will give you control, feel and touch. After all a racket as light as this should be held like a surgical scalpel rather than a bludgeon.

BADMINTON

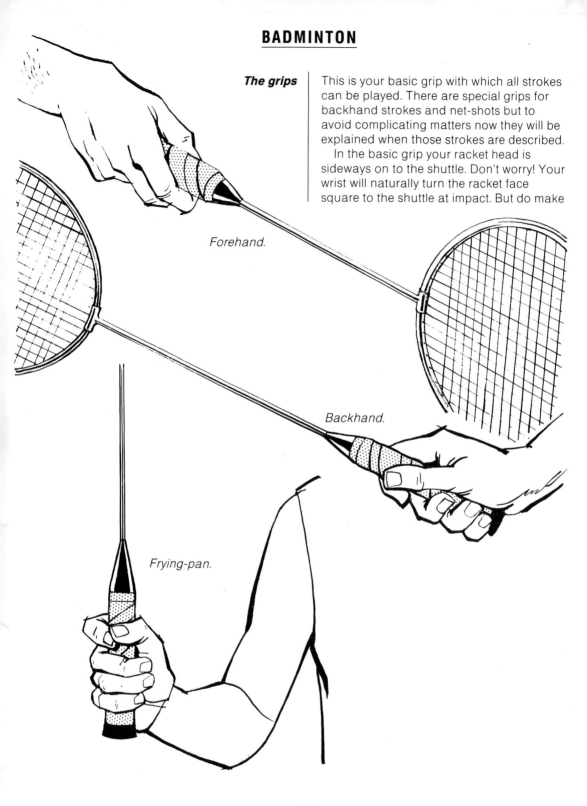

The grips | This is your basic grip with which all strokes can be played. There are special grips for backhand strokes and net-shots but to avoid complicating matters now they will be explained when those strokes are described.

In the basic grip your racket head is sideways on to the shuttle. Don't worry! Your wrist will naturally turn the racket face square to the shuttle at impact. But do make

Forehand.

Backhand.

Frying-pan.

sure you do this by turning your wrist – *not* by turning the racket handle in your hand. This will give you what for obvious reasons is called a 'frying-pan grip'. In its wake it generally brings a square stance and a weak dabbing action. That's a badminton crime! You have been warned!

Do keep checking your grip to ensure you avoid this pitfall. Remember also not to hold the racket too tightly. Be neither limp fish nor bench-vice. In the former case you will lack power, touch and control, In the latter, zip and a flexible and deceptive wrist. In between strokes, the grip may be relaxed but at impact it must be firm.

The serves

Badminton, like tennis, can boast a wide and exciting variety of serves. Unlike tennis, it cannot indulge in the easy luxury of hitting *downwards* thunderbolts at a receiver over 24m (80ft) away. The Laws of Badminton are particularly restrictive where the serve is concerned. They effectively outlaw brute strength and force the server to rely on millimetre accuracy – and trickery.

They are too, unfortunately, one of the game's few bones of contention, ones that lead to bitterness or dispute because the difference between 'fair' and 'foul' is minimal and extremely difficult to discern with absolute certainty. At club level the Laws are often flouted – out of ignorance rather than intent. So restrain your natural impatience to have a crack at the high serve and first re-read the rules. (See page 20).

1 *Low serve*
2 *Drive serve*
3 *Flick serve*
4 *High serve*
5 *Very high serve*

High serve The aim of the high serve is to force your opponent back in court and to blunt his attack. However, be wary of using this serve against experienced players with strong smashes.

To play the stroke, stand sideways on with your left shoulder and foot pointing into the diagonally opposite court. For doubles, your base is near the centre-line and up to a couple of feet behind the front service line. By way of preparation, hold the shuttle, between thumb and forefinger, with outstretched arm at shoulder height, so that if dropped it would fall a foot outside your leading foot, the left one. Sway backwards so that your weight is on the back foot. With arm bent and wrist cocked, the racket is held up almost vertically behind and to the right of your thigh. Choose your target area, then simply open thumb and forefinger to allow the shuttle to drop straight, sweeping the racket down to meet it, with the heel of the hand leading, the arm straightening, the body turning square to the net, and the knees bending slightly.

Serve trajectories.

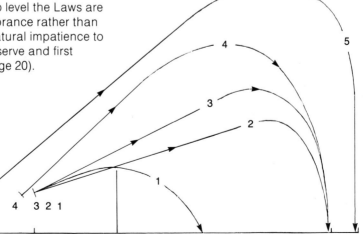

The action for the high serve.

Some 0·5m (18in) before impact give the arm a final acceleration and uncock your wrist so that at impact you are hitting hard, *upwards,* on a line with that in-the-mind's-eye target area. Keeping on that line, make a long sweep of the racket forward, up and above the left shoulder. Recover to an alert position of defensive readiness.

Do be relaxed and confident, not rigid and desperate. You're hitting the shuttle only some 9m (30ft) so there's no need to 'belt' it – just swing easily. Above all do make sure that your racket-head is under firm control at impact.

The low serve   I started you off with the high serve. This was partly because (1) it enabled you 'to feed' your partner for overhead strokes when you practised together and (2) partly because against fellow beginners without a hard smash it can be an effective serve – but not against experienced players. Against them an alternative must be found. This then is the low serve, the bread and butter serve of the game.

The aim of the low serve is to strike the shuttle with the flattest possible trajectory, so that it starts to drop just before crossing and literally skimming the tape and therefore cannot be hit down. The need for such millimetre accuracy? Not yet, but in years to come, your receiver will be standing toe to service line with his racket held menacingly within 1.5m (5ft) of that tape. With a single lunge he can demolish a still rising shuttle. So learn now to keep it low!

As with the high serve, stand sideways on, facing the receiver diagonally. So, with left foot and shoulder forward, stand tall, weight slightly on the back foot. Hold the shuttle's skirt at the top between forefinger and thumb with arm bent so that when released the shuttle will drop just to the right of your leading foot.

With the right hand, hold the racket in the conventional grip. Ensure that your grip is relaxed – not too tight and not too loose. Place the racket, pointing downwards, just to the right of and slightly behind the right thigh. No power is needed so a longer

backswing is not required. Bend the arm as far as you comfortably can to bring the racket-head up vertically as high as possible. This will give you a flatter trajectory. And the wrist is firmly cocked back – *and kept cocked back throughout the stroke*. Now, choose your target area, relax and take your time.

BADMINTON

The low serve.

Looking only at the shuttle, sway forward and gently but firmly, arm bent, wrist still cocked, *push* the shuttle forward. Don't *hit* it – stroke it, coax it. Impact is made just below hip height. Don't stop there. Push forward flat and on line, as if reluctant for racket and shuttle to part company, to waist height. With the shuttle now irretrievably on its way, step forward, and raise your racket ━ intimidatingly tape-high. You are ready to deal with any quick return to the net. Don't forget to practise this as part and parcel of your service, which after all, is the foundation of your game.

The flick serve 'But if I always serve low, won't my opponent anticipate it?' I hear you say. Dead right! He will. So you must have a surprise up your sleeve so that he is never quite certain. That surprise is the 'flick' – a last fraction-of-a-second, crisp lofting of the shuttle instead of yet another low serve. Hopefully it will wrong-foot your opponent, forcing a weak, smashable return or score an outright glorious winner.

The action? It must be a surprise, a look-alike, if it is to survive. So it is played in every way *exactly* like the low service. But, a foot – no more – before impact, the wrist you kept so unfalteringly locked back to secure a flat trajectory in the low serve, is crisply uncocked. The shuttle rises – but only just high enough to escape the unraised racket – and drops near the back doubles service line. The low service is played with the wrist cocked back throughout; the 'flick' *with* a flick of the wrist.

The drive serve   This is another variant of the low serve for sparing and surprise use. Its aim is to hit the shuttle fast, and as flat as the Laws permit, into a gap or at a vulnerable target such as the face or a weak backhand in the right court.

To be effective it must have speed and surprise. So once again it is played exactly like the low serve until just a foot before impact when the slow moving right hand is suddenly speeded up. But to keep the trajectory flattish, and so less vulnerable, the wrist must be kept cocked back as in the low serve.

The angled drive serve   This is a variant of a variant . . . of the drive serve. To gain a still wider angle, move your serving base from near the centre-line to the doubles side-line. Place your feet carefully, so that you are not infringing the rules by standing on a line. The right foot is placed right up to it, the left, a little further forward and away from it.

Again, your left shoulder points to the diagonally opposite corner. The shuttle is, however, held as far out over the side-line as is consistent with remaining on balance. This gives you a still wider angle of attack. Once again, simply jab towards the backhand target areas – powerfully.

The very high serve   Your aim with this serve is to hit the shuttle as high as strength and roof allow. To do this simply employ the technique already outlined for the high serve but use your wrist rather more fiercely and sweep rather more strongly upwards, using body-turn to the full. Take care to avoid hitting the roof!

Backhand low serve   Neither the high nor the very high serve are often played backhanded, the drive serve only infrequently. So forget them. Do, however, remember and practise the backhand low serve – and flick too, of course. They must always be considered together, for one without the other is of little use. The backhand low serve provides an admirable alternative to the forehand version.

As with all backhand strokes, use the backhand grip, thumb *behind* the handle, and point the right foot forward – right up to the front service line. The left is a little behind and to one side. Hold the shuttle, arm

The backhand serve.

straight, at about 45° just below the top of your hip, well in front of your stomach. With right arm well bent and wrist cocked, place the racket-head vertically, immediately behind the shuttle. Your elbow is high. It may seem a little awkward but you'll soon get used to it. Backswing completed.

Now, relax and select your target area, as usual. Then draw the racket back as long or as short a distance as you like – right back to your body or a matter of mere inches. Without pause, your backswing becomes your forward swing, though 'push' is again a more accurate description. Simply extend the bent forearm, *keeping the wrist cocked,* to make contact with the shuttle 0·5m (18in) in front of the body, just below hip height. Follow through quite gently for just a foot or

so to dispatch the shuttle on its net-skimming way. Then, smartly, bend the arm upwards to bring the racket-head to tape level and move in to the net. There are four distinct advantages to this serve:

1 The shuttle is struck 0·5m (18in) in front of the front service line not 0·6 (2ft) behind it: a saving of nearly 1·2 in valuable metres (4ft). This gives your opponent some 20 per cent less time to move in to attack.

2 White shuttle held directly in front of white sweater is more difficult to spot quickly than white shuttle held slightly to one side, against, perhaps, a green or brown background.

3 The forward swing is very short. The margin of error is therefore reduced.

Trajectories of smashes

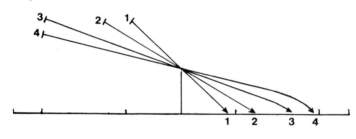

1 *from net.*
2 *from mid-court.*
3 *from doubles back service line, steeply angled.*
4 *too flat and deep.*

Trajectories of clears

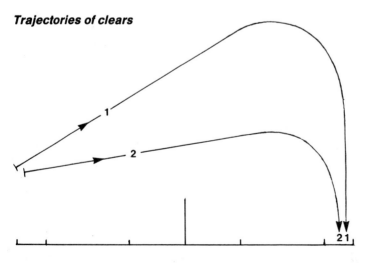

1 *defensive.*
2 *attacking.*

4 Even today, quite a number of players have not been on its receiving end before. Consequently, rather like a 'googly' at cricket, it holds a certain daunting threat.

Backhand flick serve Strangely, this, unless you have a strong wrist, is the one snag with the backhand low serve if played with a short backswing! For that, coupled with a weak wrist will make it impossible for it to achieve sufficient height to escape early interception – and annihilation. A longer backswing will help. And that, together with an average wrist, should just do the trick.

Once again, for deception, the flick must be played exactly like the low serve. Remember, whatever backswing you have for one you must have for the other. Remember too, the added power needed, as with the forehand version, must stem solely from late wrist action not early, and easily detectable, faster or longer arm action. Follow through is minimal and recovery quick. It's called a 'flick' service. That's just what it is!

Forehand overhead strokes

Since points are rarely won by just hitting the shuttle upwards, and since badminton sports a 1·5m (5ft) high net compared with the 0·9m (3ft) one of tennis and the 48cm (19in) high 'tin' of squash, the majority of shots are played overhead. It is therefore essential that you are strong in this branch of the game. And the good news is that if you can *throw* as opposed to *push* you are off to a flying start. In the former action a bent arm is powerfully snapped straight; in the latter, it remains bent and therefore lacks that essential extra snap.

There are three main overhead strokes: the defensive clears and the attacking drop-shots and smashes. Even though the clear is defensive, we will tackle it first because it is in some ways the simplest of the three – and we want early success. All strokes consist of three main phases:

1 Preparation As in all activities sound preparation is the all important foundation. In it are included *movement* to the shuttle and the *backswing* which leaves the striker actually ready to hit the shuttle.

2 Execution Sounds a little unpleasant, but this is the meat of the stroke, the vital make or break part of it. It consists of the *forward swing* and the actual *impact* with the shuttle.

3 Completion If not as exciting as 'execution', just as important. The *follow through* finally launches the shuttle under control and on-target. The *recovery* sends you quickly on your way to the next stroke . . .

Defensive clear Now to turn these general terms into specific actions. First, however, understand the purpose of the clear. It is a shot hit high and deep to the back line of your opponent's court. High, partly in order to avoid early interception and probably annihilation, and partly to give you time to recover safely back to your base; deep, to the base-line itself to blunt the effectiveness of your opponent's returns. It is a get-you-out-of-difficulties, a good-enough-to-be-getting-on-with shot.

And it depends on *length* – a word to be borne in mind at all times. A shuttle, unlike a tennis ball, decelerates very fast. So a shuttle struck from the very back of the court will, when you receive it, be travelling shorter or more slowly than one struck from 0·6m (2ft) further forward. It will, therefore, be more easily returnable.

So to the actual playing of a clear. You are, as we have already seen, mid-court in a position of readiness. As soon as you spot the flight of the shuttle to the back of your court you must obviously dance back two or three paces to position yourself sideways on so that if you allowed the shuttle to drop it would fall on your back foot (*Movement*). At the same time raise your racket directly upwards and drop it down over your right

BADMINTON

Points of impact and the 'zip' area.

shoulder to scratch your back when the shuttle is just reaching its highest point. To do this your elbow is bent and your wrist cocked back (*Backswing*).

So you are now sideways, with your weight on the back foot and your knees slightly bent. As the shuttle starts to drop throw the racket upwards with the heel of the hand leading. At the same time spiral your body upwards to put your full weight into the shot. Some 0·5m (18in) before impact uncock the wrist strongly but not fully, still hitting upwards (*Execution*). Make impact with the shuttle with a straight arm just to the right and just in front of your head. The racket-head is still angled upwards at 45° to obtain height with maximum length (*Impact*).

Now sweep the racket down to about waist height but keeping it on line to give the shuttle a last 'push' to its destined target area (*Follow through*). Even as the racket is thus sweeping down, you, well-balanced, are heading back to base, hopefully to arrive there before your opponent can actually hit your return (*Recovery*). A well-played shot – and you are ready to play another equally good one.

Enough 'do's' to last you some time. Concentrate on these and you won't need the following 'Don'ts'. However I include them to help you realize where, on occasions, you've gone wrong.

So *don't* fail to get behind the shuttle or your clear will be all height and no length. *Don't* delay your backswing until the shuttle has actually begun to fall. That way your shot will be hurried and, without straight arm impact, lacking in power. *Don't*, above all other errors, push the racket forward instead of throwing it upwards. Lack of height and power will be the result. *Don't* fail to put your body into the shot as well as arm and wrist. *Don't* uncock your wrist too early or too late. *Don't* let your racket-head waver by a sudden relaxation of grip, turn of the wrist, or loss of balance at impact or your shot won't be on target. And *don't* stand there admiring

your shot or you'll be in a whole heap of trouble with your next one. For the not too fastidious, it may help to remember key-words 'scratch!' and 'throw-up!'

Attacking clear   There are circumstances and techniques when the defensive clear can be changed into an attacking clear. It is a slightly advanced stroke – not difficult in technique, but too rarely used at club level through lack of tactical forethought rather than inability.

The circumstances for its use are when you are well-placed and on balance at the back of the court while your opponent, lured into the net by drop-shots, is still reeling back off-balance and there is an inviting gap behind him. Or, when your smash has proved unavailing and a well-dug-in defender is clearly expecting yet another smash. Or even when defensive clears of impeccable length have forced your opponent into a belated and apparently irreversible race to recover to his central base.

So with your opponent off-balance or with a gap behind him, use your attacking clear. For deception and ease of technique play it exactly like your defensive clear. Except that . . . your point of impact is now more in front of your head and at impact your racket is angled upwards only very slightly. Your resultant punched shot therefore flies fast and almost flat, but just out of your opponent's despairing reach, to the unguarded space at the back of the court. You are well placed and in no need of time to recover so it is your turn to make your opponent hurry and to gain a satisfying outright winner or force a weak return.

The drop-shot (slow)   In contrast, the delicate and attacking drop-shot gives a big return for a small expenditure of energy. It is a shot played, like the defensive clear, from between the two back lines. Although it is hit gently it is an attacking shot because it is hit *down*, not up. Its aim, the converse of the

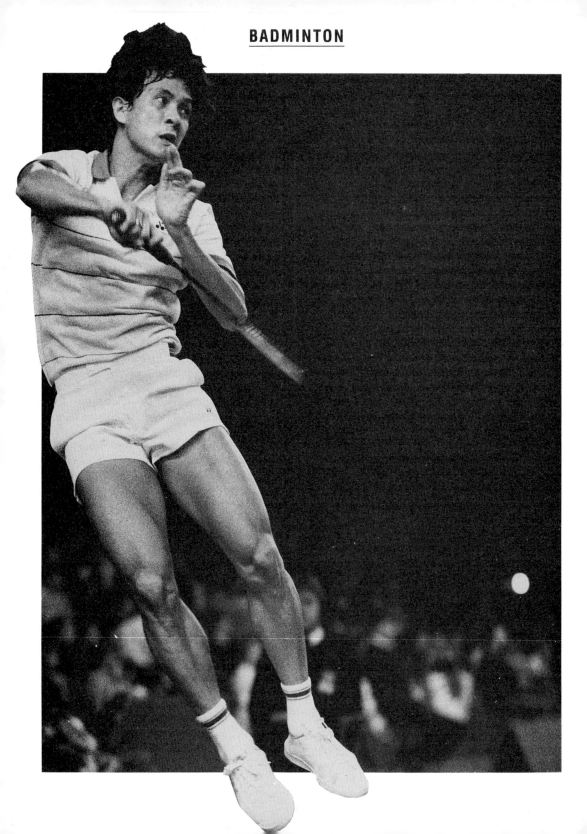

clear's, is to draw your opponent as far forward in court towards the net as possible to create a possible opening behind him, or to attack him as he hurriedly retreats, off-balance. The nearer the shuttle can be dropped to the net, the quicker it gets there and the further your opponent has to advance – and retreat.

Play it therefore exactly as you do a clear and so take your opponent by surprise. The only differences are that your point of impact is now just in front of your head, your arm speed is dramatically reduced in its last 0·5m (18in) before impact, and the shuttle is gently but firmly hit down to fall no further back in your opponent's court than his front service-line. Anything deeper than that will present him with no difficulties in returning it or recovering to base. Gradually, learn to drop it shorter . . . and shorter . . . and . . .

Cautions! The drop-shot at its best is a delicate and beautiful shot. As such it must be safeguarded by deception, for if it is spotted early for what it is, it has no defences. You must therefore make a *full* backswing and a forceful stroke to within 0·5m (18in) of impact. Above all you must hit *down,* and don't overuse the shot to the exclusion of others.

The drop-shot (fast)   This is played exactly like the slow drop-shot except that it is hit a little harder to drop about 1·2–1·5m (4–5ft) behind the front service line. It is much used in mixed doubles when there is a lady ready waiting at the net to destroy a slow drop.

The smash   The third and most important by far of the three overhead shots. The most satisfying too, for it is the power shot, the shot that by sheer speed scorches through your opponent's defence. It is the clincher of rallies, the winner of points, the climax of a dozen previous shots.

Killer instinct! Liem Swie King of Indonesia smashes at full power.

It is played with much the same action, the throwing action, which you have already mastered in the clears and the drop-shot. All three must be played similarly up to the last fraction of a second so that each is invested with deception as well as its own particular qualities.

It differs from the clear only in these respects. You must position yourself *further behind* the shuttle since you are going to take it earlier and some 0·5m (18in) in front of your face. At impact the wrist fully – and powerfully – uncocks so that the racket face is directed downwards. And because of this downward sweep the follow through is longer, down past the legs. But not so long that the racket cannot be quickly brought into action again to kill off the weak reply elicited. On occasions you will score an outright winner with your first shot. On others, your smash is only the first of a barrage, each eliciting a slightly shorter and shorter reply until after perhaps three or four smashes you can adminster the *coup de grâce.*

'Don'ts' are mercifully few – but only because they have already been largely dealt with under 'the clear'. Don't be sluggish in your footwork. Don't attempt to gain power by brute strength alone; remember that it is best achieved by the perfect synchronization of each phase of the shot in a steadily rising crescendo of speed – by timing. And never let the shuttle drop in the vain hope that you can hit it harder at head-level than at full-arm stretch. Remember the old physics law – the longer the lever, the greater the power exerted.

Remember, too, that in these days of light racket manoeuvrability and fast reactions, speed alone will not always gain the day. To be fully effective it needs three allies. The first is *steepness.* The hardest smash hit flat but not downwards can be attacked, driven downwards. If it is hit steeply, by means of straight arm and crisply uncocked wrist, the return must be lifted. The hunt is still on! The second is *placement.* The smash should

The action for the smash.

never be a wildly swung blow: it should be directed to the badminton point of the jaw, the inner hip, to elicit a cramped reply; or to the badminton *solar plexus,* a gap from which the shuttle will not be returned. And the third is *consistency.* It gains you nothing to achieve one rabble-rousing outright winner if the next two tear holes in the bottom of the net or spread alarm amongst side-line spectators.

Backhand strokes

We all have our weaknesses, and in badminton it is generally in playing

backhand shots, i.e. those where the shuttle is struck on the left-hand side of the right-hander's body – with the back of the hand to the net. This is not as natural an action as that used on the forehand, and consequently is weaker and more subject to error.

The backhand therefore is a two-faced coin. Knowing it is likely to be a weakness, opponents will make a ploy of hitting the shuttle to your left. You must therefore regularly practise backhand strokes to eliminate such a weakness. Conversely, of course, you must hit to your opponent's left-hand side, especially in the rear court, rather than to his forehand side.

As a backhand stroke even when frequently practised is often still weaker than a forehand one, it is better to avoid playing such a shot at all when the shuttle is hit high and deep. This can be done in two ways: (1) by running round the shot and, (2) by playing round-the-head strokes.

Round-the-head strokes Too often a shot even a foot or so to a player's left seems to mesmerize him either into inaction or to a timid attempt at a weak backhand stroke. If you are in an alert position of readiness it is easy enough to skip or chassé a couple of paces to the left so that the shuttle is now just to your right and can be played forehanded and more powerfully. Quite simple, isn't it?

Even if the shuttle is 0·9–1·2m (3–4ft) to your left there is still the opportunity to avoid using a backhand stroke. It is too far away for you to play it forehanded as just described. Instead you will play a round-the-head stroke in the following way.

Chassé, or turn and run, across court to as near its line of flight as possible. At the same time prepare your stroke normally by dropping the racket-head over your shoulder to the 'scratch' position. Now you are only one or two feet to the right of the shuttle and square to it. Make a final long sideways stride by placing your left foot well out to the left. Don't throw the racket normally (i.e. straight forward to the right of the head), because the shuttle isn't there. Instead, as you lean well out to the left, bring it across your head to hit the shuttle, still with the forehand face of your racket, 30–60cm (12–24in) to the left of your shoulder. Your forearm actually brushes the top of your head.

Leaning well out to the left like this you are now something of a Leaning Tower of Pisa. By placing the left foot well out to the left, try to maintain balance or you will be dangerously out of position. By thrusting off hard with it, make a quick recovery to centre court.

With this ploy you can play forehanded clears, drop-shots, or smashes, as previously described. However, you can dodge backhand strokes up to a point, but you can't eliminate them altogether.

Backhand strokes in general First a few rough rules of thumb for all such strokes, before we consider them individually:

1 The basic grip may be used, but a specialized grip will probably give you added power and control. To achieve this hold the racket in the basic forehand grip. Relax that grip and with your fingers turn the racket

The round-the-head-smash.

some 30° to the right. You can now place your thumb flat along what is going to be the *back* bevel of the handle. This will give you extra leverage and control. Practise this change from forehand to backhand and back again off-court until it is automatic. In play, it will require no conscious thought. It will just happen.

2 The right foot is always placed towards the shuttle's line of flight.

3 At the same time bring the right hand near the left shoulder (arm bent; wrist cocked back) so that the racket may be thrown flat, down or up at the shuttle.

4 Begin the forward swing by thrusting the right elbow 'into' the shuttle, then wrist, and racket.

Let's start with the simple lob and work our way up to the crowning glories of the overhead strokes.

Backhand lob The lob is an underhand stroke used to return a shuttle which is well below tape-level, in the forecourt. Its aim is to hit the shuttle high and deep to the back of the court to give you time to regain your control base and to blunt your opponent's attack. In other words it is the underhand counterpart of the clear.

The backhand lob.

Move to the shuttle taking a final long lunge so that you are not cramped and keep your back foot near base. Point the right foot at the drop of the shuttle. Bring the racket to the left side of the body with right hand by left shoulder, and racket, by means of bent arm and bent wrist, held vertically at shoulder level. Sweep the racket-head down with the elbow leading, the arm straightening and, in the 'zip' area, wrist uncocking to make impact just to the left of the leading foot. Let the racket flow with straight arm above head level on line with the target area. Recover quickly to your position of readiness by thrusting off strongly with the bent right leg.

Remember you are hitting the shuttle only just half the length of the court so 'lean on it', stroke it, rather than hit it. Be all elegance and grace. If the shuttle is dropping very near the net you will have to angle up your racket face to give the shuttle's flight the necessary verticality to clear the net. Remember too, unless you wish to experience the ignominy of a shuttle in the face as you retreat, that *length, height and recovery* are the Three Virtues.

Backhand drive   The drive is a splendid attacking shot, hit fast and flat generally down the sidelines. It is used mainly in mixed doubles by the male player.

All the principles previously mentioned apply again. This time however instead of diagonally facing the net you are sideways on to it. The right foot points directly at the sideline, slightly distanced from it so that the shuttle can be struck at full arm's-length. Right hand is again by left shoulder, but the racket shaft is horizontal to the ground and virtually across the shoulder.

Fling the racket-head at the shuttle, arm straightening, body turning, wrist uncocking, to make impact just in front of the body. If the shuttle is at tape level the racket-head will be absolutely vertical to produce a flat, net-skimming shot. (If the shuttle is slightly below, the racket-head is very slightly angled up; if above, down.) Lean into the shot so that you can keep the racket-head square to the shuttle and flat as long as possible to drive it down the side-line. (To play a cross-court shot meet the shuttle 0·5m (18in) *in front of* the body and hit across court.) Follow through to above the right shoulder and, pushing on the right foot, recover quickly. Remember, do get that right foot across.

Danish wipe or Swedish swish   These are a cross between drive and lob. Played from the back of the court, the shuttle is allowed to drop to waist height. Drive action is used but instead of a flat swing the racket is swept

BADMINTON

The backhand drive.

down then up under the shuttle to loft it right to the baseline. Use plenty of 'wipe', body action, and 'swish', wrist action. Its disadvantages compared with the overhead clear are that by letting the shuttle drop, downward angle and variety of shot are sacrificed. Worse still your opponent is given time!

How to play the 'Danish wipe'.

TECHNIQUE

Overhead backhand strokes The most elegant and apparently effortless of strokes as the power ones rely largely on use of the wrist and timing. But they need a commensurate amount of practice. Clear, drop-shot and smash can all be played as with the forehand.

Same old principles . . . So, pivoting on your left foot, almost turn your back on the net (though still watching the shuttle carefully over your shoulder) and point your right foot to the left hand, back corner 'box'.

At the same time, right hand yet again to left shoulder, arm bent, elbow up, wrist cocked so that the racket-head is roughly on a level with the small of your back. Bend the knees slightly, spiral the body upwards, snap the arm straight, uncock the wrist and make upward impact just in front of the head. Since so much of the stroke's power is in the

Steve Baddeley has his wrist thrust forward so as to better control the racket head for this drop shot at the net.

Playing a backhand clear.

wrist snap, this must be very exactly timed – neither too early nor too late – but within the 'zip' area 0·5m (18in) each side of the impact point.

For the *smash,* impact is some 0·5m (18in) in front of the head. And as the backhand smash is very much less powerful than the forehand you should not attempt it from further back than mid-court, from where it can be an efficient snap-shot. As an alternative from deeper in court there is still the drop-shot, in which the wrist is gently rolled over to make impact in front of the head.

Side arm strokes (forehand)

The drive This is a side-arm stroke played flat and fast down the sidelines. Its aim is to gain a weak return or a winner by driving the shuttle fast into a player's body or into a gap left fleetingly uncovered. It is used mainly by the male, from a mid-court position, in mixed doubles.

As an analogy it is played with somewhat the same action as that used by cover-point at cricket or by a person skimming stones along the surface of still water. To this end, chassé to your right then take a further long step across so that you are sideways on with your feet in line pointing at right angles to the sideline. At the same time prepare your stroke by drawing the racket back at shoulder height so that by bending your arm and cocking the wrist the racket-head is brought back almost between your shoulder-blades. Your body weight is still mainly on the back foot.

Fling the racket-head out towards the shuttle by snapping the arm straight and uncocking the wrist in the 'zip' area. But at the same time turn your body square to the net and let your weight flow into the shot and onto the front foot. With racket-head angled slightly down if the shuttle is above

The backhand smash.

The forehand drive.

the tape, and at right-angles to the floor if it is level with it, make impact at full arm stretch just in front of the body. This maximizes power and minimizes the distance you have to recover to get back to base.

The push This stroke is played with exactly the same action as the drive – for the sake of deception. But the shuttle is struck with only half the force so that it drops *between* net-player and back-player. The 'power' action hopefully deters the former from attempting to intercept the comparatively slow moving shuttle.

BADMINTON

The drop-shot   This stroke is played threateningly like the drive until just before impact when arm and wrist speed are both considerably slowed down to hit the shuttle only just over the net. Because the shuttle is travelling so slowly it may be necessary to angle the racket-head slightly up to overcome the pull of gravity tending to drag it down into the net.

And again because of its vulnerable slowness of flight it should be played only when both opponents are mid-court or the net-player is slow, off-balance or positioned too far behind the front service line.

Net-shots

Net-shots are shots played *from* near the net, and often, very near *to* the net. They can be hit down or up. The latter, requiring a featherlight touch, may travel no more than an inch upwards and forwards and yet win a point outright as surely as a heavyweight smash. It is this combination of sheer power and delicate touch that helps to make badminton such a fascinating game.

Upward net-shots   These shots are played as returns of drop-shots or of your opponent's net-shots. Your aim is twofold: to return them so close to the tape that your opponent cannot hit them down; and so tight to the net that your opponent will find it difficult to play the shuttle without hitting the net and, even if he does so, to get sufficient angle to hit it to a good length. A net-shot, therefore, hopefully gains an outright winner or forces a weak net return or a lob that can be killed. Ideally it grazes the tape and topples immediately down touching the net as it falls.

To play these stand at about an angle of 45° to the net with the right foot forward. With racket arm extended and almost straight try and make impact as early and high as possible. Take the shuttle at tape-height if you can and it will almost bounce off your racket without any action by

The backhand net shot: watching the shuttle intently on to the very strings.

you. Take it a foot lower and it will need only minimal action, a delicate upward caress, not a blow.

For all the delicacy, it is a perfect stroke in miniature, one played with back- and forward-swing and follow through all within a compass of a mere 23cm (9in).

If you are late in intercepting the shuttle, you will obviously take it well below tape-level. And if it is so tight to the net that you cannot play it without hitting the net as well, you will have to let it fall below the level of the bottom of the net. In these cases you will have to sweep it strongly upwards.

Downward net-shots Obviously it is far better to hit down for a fairly certain winner than hit up for a more problematical one. To be able to hit down you must take the shuttle earlier still. And to do that you must be on your toes, quick to spot a weak shot to the net, and bubbling with aggression.

To that end therefore stand, better still bounce a little, square to the net, with your racket up-raised at tape-height in front of your right shoulder, in a 'frying-pan grip' or the basic grip.

The frying-pan grip almost speaks for itself! In it the racket is held square on, not sideways, to the net, with the palm directly behind the handle. It is a good grip for dabbing down as it enables the net-player to play shuttles on either side, backhand or forehand, without changing grips. It does however necessitate a quick change of grip if an upward shot has to be played. It should never be used at the back court as it inhibits the all-important use of the wrist.

With the grip decided on, all that is needed at the net is a dabbing action. You have no time – and no need of a full

'scratch' backswing, so do not bring the racket back further than your ears. Impact is a little in front of the body just above tape-height, when the bent forearm has been extended a little and the wrist has been crisply uncocked. The latter action is essential if the shuttle is to be hit steeply down. Failure to use the wrist leads only to a flat and easily returnable push. Or, if struck with real venom, to the shuttle still gathering speed as it flies out over the base-line. Over-ambitious use can drag the shuttle down into the net. So aim for a happy medium that places it on the floor about mid-court.

Playing a forehand at the net.

The return of serve stance.

that eight times out of ten you eventually win the rally. You will achieve this very desirable position if you really think out the following points.

Position in court Your aim is to meet every serve, low or high, while it is above the tape. You must therefore so position yourself that you can reach both in time to attack them. A top-class player, very fit and agile, can stand right up to the front service line knowing that he can spring backwards and kill high or flick serves. This is your ideal too – but not yet. Try standing some 1 to 1·5m (3–5ft) from the front service line according to how quick or slow you are moving backwards. Remember that once you have developed a reasonably strong smash, serves to you will, wisely, generally be low. So make certain you can meet those before they drop below tape-level.

So stand, or rather crouch, 0·9m (3ft) behind the front service line. And, in the right court, within 0·3 or 0·4m (1–1½ft) of the centre line to cover your backhand.

In the left-hand court you will still be 0·9m (3ft) back but you will have moved your position some 0·9m (3ft) more away from the centre line. Your aim here is to cover your weaker backhand to some extent but to be quite sure you can still attack anything down the centre line.

In the final analysis only you, knowing your own speed, greyhound-quick or cab-horse slow, can decide exactly where you stand. Err on the side of optimism because you *must* be able to attack low serves. If you're caught by one or two flick serves it doesn't matter providing you are crunching the low ones. If you are caught by more than one or two you'll have to drop back – and hate it.

The great Kirsten Larsen of Denmark, in action at the Yonex All England Open Championship. This is a typically athletic stroke.

Recovery of the racket-head is very important. You are hitting the shuttle crisply to a near target. If it is returned, it will fly back equally fast. So immediately the short follow through is ended, for fear of hitting the net, have the racket up-raised again.

Return of serve

Just as important as the serve itself! If you serve well, particularly if you get the lift, you could well win most of the following rallies. If you return well, you make it very difficult for your opponents to score points. A very pleasing combination.

The aim of the return of serve is either to score a winner outright or to achieve so commanding a position with the first stroke

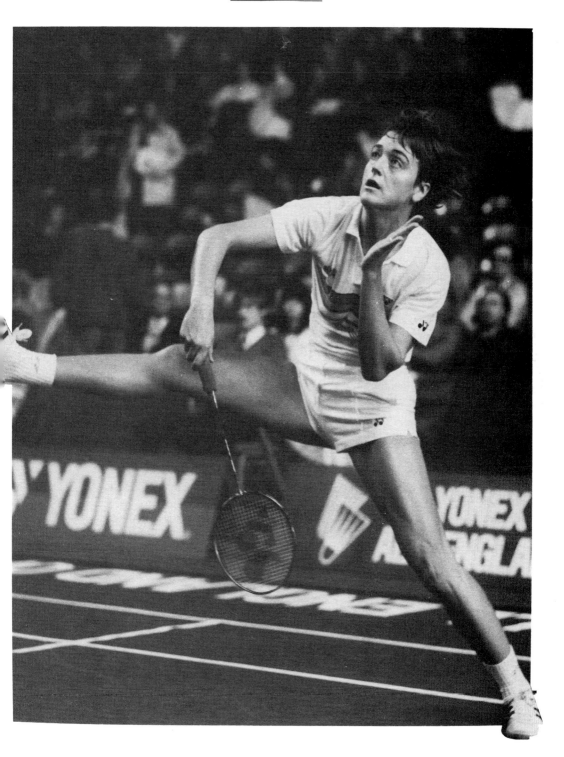

BADMINTON

Stance It is important to position yourself exactly to be able to attack both low and high serves. It is equally important how you stand. You must be quick off the mark!

To that end take up a sprinter's starting position. Left foot forward, right foot stretched out behind in a long crouch. You are on the balls of both feet. That way you can push off quickly backwards from the front foot, and equally quickly forwards from the back foot. Your left knee is well bent, your right rather less so. Your weight is on the left foot so that you are leaning slightly forwards, for that is the direction in which you will travel the majority of times. Your racket-head is held at head-level, slightly forward of the body, ready for instant action. Your left hand is at the same level, still further forwards. You aren't a smiling upright kindly figure. You are a scowling, crouching, threatening predator. Intimidate your opponent – look threatening!

Return of the smash

We have seen that the smash is the most powerful shot in your armoury. And doubtless too in that of your opponent's. So, how to counter it? Your constant aim in badminton, and not only with the smash, is to turn defence into attack.

Returning a shuttle hit hard and travelling fast demands several qualities – coolness, concentration, observation, fast reflexes and racket manoeuvrability. Sounds a tall order, but if you take one thing at a time it's not as difficult as it sounds. And there is great satisfaction to be obtained from nonchalantly returning your opponent's best thunderbolts.

Whenever you lift a shuttle to the back of the court (but do it as rarely as possible) immediately prepare for trouble. Too many players lack urgency – not panic, but urgency. And yet the shuttle will be whistling back at them in a split second.

Position and stance Coolly drop back to mid-court to take some of the speed off the shuttle and make your task a little simpler. Generally position yourself nearly square to the net but with the right foot slightly forward. Your racket, in a backhand grip, should be angled so that the head is up in front of your stomach – a likely target. In such a position you are immediately ready to counter shots straight into the body. And your racket-head is equidistant from shots to either side, so leaving no glaring gap. Don't dig in to resist the 'shock', but rather be on your toes because your tricky opponent may not smash at all – but rather see if you are alert with a well-disguised attacking clear or drop-shot.

Watch that action Well positioned and armoured, you now concentrate solely on your opponent's action to try and spot early whether it's his action for smash – or drop.

How to stand prior to returning a smash.

If it is the former, now observe his racket-head closely to see whether, at impact, it is aimed at your body, to the left or to the right. Then from his racket-head pick up the line of flight of the actual shuttle. And follow it onto your very strings. If you can discern the line of flight *early* you give yourself an extra vital split second in which to play a coolly measured stroke. If you don't see the shuttle's line until it is crossing the net, panic and hasty error will ensue. So, spot the shuttle early!

The push or block If the shuttle is hit to one side of your body you have little time for any real backswing. Nor do you need it. For you merely place the racket to the side under pressure, just behind the body. Then, with wrist locked and racket-head tilted slightly up, push the racket slightly forward to 'block' the shuttle back, angled and fast enough to avoid net interception. The same applies to a shot aimed at your body which should be played backhanded. But the backswing will be limited – by your stomach.

The drive Playing just one type of return invites anticipation and interception, so learn other returns. This is virtually the same stroke as the push played with a little more backswing and therefore harder, which pre-supposes you are now spotting the shuttle earlier and so have time for that slightly longer backswing. It is hit fast directly at the smasher before he has time to fully recover from his power-shot – or to the opposite side of the court to hurry him into error.

Net-shot This is a third alternative. Played much as for the 'block' but the backswing is almost entirely eliminated. The shuttle bounces off the racket, held in a relaxed grip, to drop just over the net. Very dangerous against a forward and active net-player, but a possibility against one who stands back for the drive or is sluggish. Very useful in singles.

Crouch defence Contrastingly agressive and only for those who like to take the fight to the enemy. All depends on your opponent's speed and steepness of smash – and *your* reflexes.

If his cross-court smash tends to be *flat*, move into the front service line, and crouch down diagonally opposite the smasher. You are now some 1·5–1·8m (5–6ft) further forward than the norm and the shuttle may well be travelling 38km/h (20mph) faster there than when further back even though it is on the longer cross-court line.

Make sure therefore that your racket is raised head-high even before your opponent strikes the shuttle. If you are frightened of being hit in the face, hold the racket in front of it, and look through the strings. At this close range you will have time only to 'dab' the shuttle down with a slight forward movement of the forearm and a slight uncocking of the wrist. It really is a 'kill' or 'be killed' shot.

The lob A last resort. This is played like the lob already described though the long lunge is going to be unnecessary. Indeed it can best be likened to the high service. It demands quick reflexes and racket manoeuvreability because, from the basic defensive position of readiness, the racket must be swung back just behind the thigh. It is then swept down to meet the shuttle by the leading foot. Use of the wrist will help loft it to the back of the court – and with essential 'timing' minimize the amount of power needed. You will find that top players play the same stroke merely by use of a very whippy wrist and forearm.

But whichever technique is adopted nothing alters the fact that you are hitting *up*. Return smash after smash in this way – but you are still defending. Your opponents are still attacking. The status quo has not been altered. So, in defence your motto is 'Keep it flat! Regain the attack.' Nobody can successfully base their defensive game on the lob – it's just too risky!

GAME · TACTICS

Court courtesies

Badminton, like all other sports, has its code of good manners. As they are as much a part of the game as 'service' or 'smash', and as you want to start off on the right foot from the word go, I'm giving them pride of place.

In your early club days, members will ask you to play, not vice versa, or a Committee member, supervising a 'board system', will arrange your games for you. Later, when you make up your own games, don't ask the aces but rather players of roughly your own standard. When called, be ready to play and quick to go on court. But never walk across another court or even walk behind one when play is in progress.

Don't be afraid to tell your partner you are inexperienced. Without overdoing it, praise – 'Good shot' – or encourage your partner – 'Well tried'. And after a particularly poor shot of your own an occasional wry 'Sorry, partner!' doesn't come amiss. When you, or on occasions, your partner hits the shuttle into the net, retrieve it and accurately hit, throw or pass it to the server. *Never* just scoop it back hockey-fashion!

In matches it is customary to shake hands with your opponents at the end of a game but in club play 'Thank you, partner' suffices.

Badminton has always been a singularly sporting game. It certainly has no time for McEnroe-style tantrums, excuses in defeat, recriminations as to the score, or disputed line calls. In regard to the latter remember you never query your opponents' line decisions on *their* side of the net. On your side, call quickly. If there is a slight doubt give it to your opponents; a reasonable doubt and ask if a let may be played. It is solely up to you to call your own slings or touches. (See page 24.) Be absolutely fair but not quixotic.

Even if you never become the club 'tiger', you can at least achieve a reputation as a cheerful, good sport, who never gives up and who is fun to play with.

General hints (applying to doubles as well as singles)

1 By concentration and care (they go hand in hand), avoid unforced errors – bonus points for your opponent(s). An early lead raises your morale; lowers your opponent's.

2 If it is you who are down in points, never be down in spirits. With care, your turn will come.

3 Never show anger or despondency to your opponent; it's a boost to his morale, and it doesn't help yours!

4 Know the score after each rally.

5 Within the Laws and bounds of sportsmanship, slow the game down if you are losing, speed it up if you are winning.

6 Try to realize your errors of technique or tactics: and to spot and play on your opponent's.

7 If you creep up from 8-13 say, to 13 all, avoid the danger of unconsciously relaxing and finding yourself 0-3 down.

8 Similarly, at the beginning of the second game, decide on your tactics and then away again at full pressure.

9 If you're winning easily, never ease up and let your opponent(s) have a few easy points. He (they) will play better and you will find it hard to get back into the saddle again.

10 Don't rage at net-cords against you or doubtful decisions by your opponents. You merely lose concentration and play badly.

11 In doubles, 'call' for your partner. If he is racing to play a shuttle he has little time to spare to see whether it is likely to be 'in' or 'out'. You have. So call 'Yes', if likely to be in; 'No', if going to be out; and 'Watch', if it's going to be a very close thing. Call early and sharply or you will not stop in his tracks a player who is eager to have a crack at the shuttle.

12 Take time at the end of a game, or even, quickly between rallies, to point out an opponent's weakness you have spotted, or suggest an improvement in your own (or partner's) technique or tactics.

13 Be scrupulously fair.

14 Fight to the last point whatever the score.

15 Win modestly, lose cheerfully.

16 In losing, learn. After every game, be a little badminton-wiser.

SINGLES

As a novice you will find singles an excellent form of practice. However, in a one-court club your opportunities to play singles with, perhaps, a dozen other members forced to sit and watch, will be few. Try very early – or last thing. Far better, if you can, to book a sports centre court for an hour's continuous practice.

In order to play such singles you must be more than averagely fit – though, of course, the very act of playing will increase stamina and fitness. And, hopefully, create a sound range of basic strokes. If your backhand strokes from the back corner are weak you will, if your opponent is alert, be under constant pressure. From that evil, good too may eventually emerge in that you will *have to* develop round-the-head and backhand shots.

Yet another benefit is that with only one player on each side, the tempo of the game is slower, more measured. You have more time to think your shots and the tactical plan is simpler in that you have only yourself to consider. And no one else to blame when you make a mistake – or to rely on when you're in a hole!

Preliminaries

These play their part. Warm up off-court before you start, as much to get the adrenalin flowing as to avoid pulled muscles or to ensure inch-saving suppleness.

If you have choice of ends, carefully note background for vision, floor for roughness or slipperiness, or possible 'drift' due to strong draughts or heating-fans in a big hall across, up or down a court. Some players like the best end first to gain the first game and win in two 'straight'. Others, perhaps more pessimistic, take the worst end first so that in the crucial third game they have the advantage of the best end to clinch the game, or to make a dogged fight back.

In your knock-up, concentrate only on the *singles* strokes you are going to need. Conceal your weaknesses if you can. A quick show of force with withering smash or deceptive drop can be effective, but don't overdo it. Probe for your opponent's weaknesses and note his strengths. But don't let the latter worry you – many a player looks good in a knock-up but can't string his strokes together into an effective tactical whole when under pressure. Strive for concentration, length consistency, and movement.

High serve

Remember that as you are playing within the bounds of a long, narrow court your aim is to run your opponent up and down it from corner to corner and to tire him and force weak returns.

To that end, the serve in singles is high and deep to the base-line which now, in singles, is also the back service-line. From the right court aim a couple of feet to the left of the centre-line. This leaves a reasonable margin of error and cuts down your opponent's chance to cross-court disconcertingly. From the left court leave the same margin, or take the slight risk of a less

Narrowing the angle in singles: when the shuttle is hit to a, b1 is base; to b, b2 is base. to c, b3 is base.

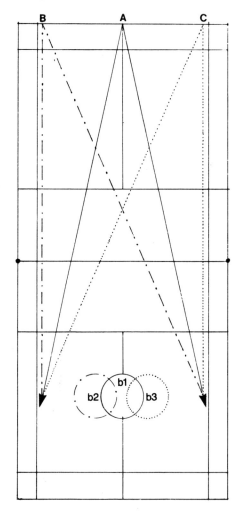

likely cross-court shot by hitting to what you hope is a frail backhand. Though, heaven knows, all such serves should be returned forehanded by virtue of neat footwork, or round-the-head strokes.

Whichever target area you thoughtfully choose and observe, remember your *length* must be full – within a foot of the base-line. Thus, at this level of play, you should have

blunted your opponent's attack; his smash will lack penetration, his clears length, and his drop-shots, urgency. And you have also opened up the forecourt for attack. Two advantages for the price of one.

Narrowing the angle   If you do decide to serve out to either corner then instead of stepping straight back, step 0·3–0·5m (12–18in) to one side of the centre line; to the left if you have served to the forehand, to the right, if to the backhand. This is called 'narrowing the angle of return'. The theory is that the majority of returns will be straight. Therefore, if you have moved as I suggest, you will be nearer such a shot and therefore faster to its return. And, provided you have not, recklessly and anticipatorily, moved *too* far, you will be able to move across quite easily to take a cross-court shot – as the shuttle has a longer flight so you have a compensating fractionally longer time in which to move to it. This movement applies equally when you clear or lob.

Low serve

The one disadvantage of such a high serve is that you have generously broken a key badminton principle by *lifting* the shuttle, so giving your opponent the attack. Top players you will notice use this high serve much more sparingly because at their level their opponent can smash and clear effectively even from so deep in court. They therefore often employ a straightforward low serve to the T-junction. So, for variety, may you. But never give up a basic tactic too early or too often. An occasional change – and then a quick return to the high serve – can be unsettling.

If your high serve is having an off day in regard to length, a low serve is an essential variant. As your opponent has to stand further back to receive than he would in doubles he is unlikely to be able to rush it. He is therefore forced to lift, to give you the chance of attack either in 'killing' his net-return or smashing his lob. And having to use a different stroke may unsettle him in length and accuracy.

But there is another point to be noted. You are serving from a deeper base than in doubles so don't carelessly serve short. And remember that if you are weak backhanded a quick lob to that corner by your opponent can land you in deep trouble. So, in play, observe closely the pros and cons that actually result from low and high serves.

Flick and drive serve can be variants for the regular low serve. Your flick, remember, must fly some 1·2m (4ft) further, so try to keep it a deceptive flick, not an obvious hit. With a receiver standing further back a drive loses some of its surprise value. Use it therefore only on a weak backhand in the right court or into a generously large gap.

Return of serve

Return of serve is as ever vitally important in that it sets the tempo of the coming rally. All that we have said previously as to position and stance applies, but to cope with a 0·76m (2ft 6in) deeper serve you will have to stand further back.

Of the low serve   If it is high over the tape dab it down into a mid-court gap near the side-line. If it is tape-skimming, hurry in to play a delicate net-shot to the corner of the net away from the server who dare not follow in as swiftly or far as he would in doubles with a partner behind him. If you are slow and your opponent follows in or has a weak backhand, then lift deceptively fast and just high enough to avoid interception to the back-line – and look for a weak return.

Of the high serve   If you have a strong clear, use it, to the backhand if your opponent is weak or sluggish and to the forehand if he covers his backhand side too much. By hitting to the forehand you open up the court, hoping to create a backhand gap that you can exploit next shot.

If your opponent is strong from the forehand deep corner then obviously hit down, attack with a drop-shot to one of the front corners. In so doing you hopefully open up the back of the court for an attacking clear.

Of other serves   Flicks should be smashed if of poor length, dropped if of good length, cleared high if you are off-balance to give you time to recover. If your reactions are quick, a drive down your backhand can be lethally returned to body or gap with a round-the-head smash. If they are slow, a blocked, or dabbed drop-shot to the corner of the net is a safe reply.

War of attrition

Singles are not as forthrightly aggressive as doubles. In the latter with your partner covering the net you can afford to go all out for winners. In singles, on your own, you must be more circumspect for there is always a lot of court to be guarded. Singles, therefore, tend to be much more a war of attrition, of probing for an opening – and, when it does occur, of sudden all-out attack to seize the hard-worked-for opportunity. So, although there is a No Man's Land when neither player is clearly on top, tactics are best divided under attack and defence.

Attack

Your main weapon is, of course, the smash. Use it sparingly for it is tiring, and should you not be on balance and in position, a quick return from your quick smash will leave you in desperate trouble.

Never, except as the rarest of surprise packets or if a gap is phenomenally large, smash from between the two back lines. It would be about as effective as hammering on a brick wall with your bare fists.

With the shuttle forced short by one of your previous succession of clears or drops, position and balance being good, go for a winner into a gap, though allow a margin of error for the down-the-side-line smash. A smash into your opponent's body, not comfortably either side onto his racket, will leave him cramped and force a weak mid-court shot you can finish off.

The slow drop-shot, for all its delicacy and lack of pace, is an attacking shot simply because, hit downwards, it forces a lift. It can be played from the base-line instead of an upwards clear. Played deceptively to the corners it can win a point outright, or, if it is tight enough, a lob short or into the net. Even if neither of these happy events takes place, used in conjunction with the deep clear it can tiringly force your opponent in and out, from side to side.

At this stage it is doubtful if your opponent will be quick or opportunist enough to risk an incursion into the net to kill it in mid-flight – always supposing you haven't generously signalled your intent by lack of backswing, grunt or grimace. Also, if you tend to play too many drops, without interspersing them with telling clears, that will cool his eagerness. If you are off-balance, a high deep clear will at least maintain the stalemate status quo. If, on the other hand, it is your opponent who is off-balance after a lob or over-eager to get into the net then a flat, fast attacking clear over his head will send him reeling back too late or only able to make a very short clear. So, all four overhead strokes, well played in the right tactical circumstances, can further your cause.

What I have said of the forehand could apply to the backhand but, let's face it, your backhand may lack length, your smash, sting. If your overhead backhand isn't up to scratch don't disdain the lustier Danish wipe until it is. You must have length. Better still, by good 'reading' – and nimble footwork – protect the frail backhand with round-the-head strokes.

When your opponent plays a drop-shot, move in early to counter it with a tight net-shot – and another and another if need be. Don't be chicken by lifting to the back, possibly short, unless your opponent is too far committed to the net and vacant acres at the back call invitingly.

Games can be won in tight net play more often than on smashes. Such net-shots may force either a mis-hit into the net, or a return a foot above the tape that you can dab crisply *down* for a winner, or a half-court clear.

A typical singles rally. The numbers represent the sequence of strokes played.

Be eager but not over-eager to score winners. Be prepared – and fit enough – to play long rallies until just the shot you need is played. Then go for the outright winner – without letting the chance slip past you.

Do not play your shots to a pattern – for example, to each corner in turn, or more simply clear, drop, clear, drop, clear . . . play two, three, four successive clears then your drop – or vice versa. Even then you needn't alternate clears to each corner in turn. It is more taxing for your opponent, running in to centre-court base, to have suddenly to slide into reverse and back-track. Keep your opponent guessing! It's wearing for him – both mentally and physically.

Defence

Your range of strokes here is more limited, less clear-cut. The high clear and lob are never likely to gain you a winner but they will gain you time to get back to base, on balance, before your opponent can play his next stroke. Remember, height is a two-edged weapon: lots of it gives you time; the minimum of it, but enough to avoid interception, will hurry your opponent.

Length, too, is essential, Try and spare a glance at your opponent's feet. If his back foot is over the back line, the shuttle will fall just about on it. If it is only over the back doubles line, your lob or clear is short, and retribution will follow. Even if you cannot find time to notice this, do realize that if your opponent's smashes suddenly seem to acquire the zing of a world-class player then that is due not to his sudden acquisition of genius but rather your loss of length.

In returning any shot, but particularly in returning smash from rear-court or dab from the net, 'be prepared'. Have your racket across body-target area, your feet moving in order to take avoiding action if there is time; and above all, your eyes watching opponent action and impact for early anticipation.

Your safest reply is a push drop-shot to the net. Alternatives? A wristy lob if the smasher is over optimistically following in, or a cross-court drive if he is off-balance.

MEN'S · AND · LADIES' · DOUBLES

Ladies' doubles were once known as 'glassy eye'. And male spectators were reputed to make a quick dash for the bar when they began. This because rallies tended to be a series of interminable defensive clears with smashes, drops, net-shots and any real action as rare as a solar eclipse.

Not so today. Anyone who has watched our top ladies athletically battling it out will agree there's plenty of action from the likes of Li Lingwei, Gillian Clark or Young Suk Lee. Rallies are still long – but fluctuating – because ladies' cast-iron defences are almost impenetrable by their comparatively lighter smashes without the aid of lightning-reflexed net interceptions.

Nevertheless, without chauvinism, it must be admitted that it is the even tougher men's doubles final that guarantees a full house and brings the crowd to its feet. See Hadibowo leap a metre (3ft) off the ground, grunting ferociously each time as he hammers down thunderbolt smashes at imperturbable Li Yongbo who, with a flick of the wrist, whips them high back to an increasingly frustrated Hadibowo. Then, with a grunt to outgrunt all grunts – a delicate drop-shot sends Tian Bingyi diving forward to retrieve it, somehow to inch it over the net where Ertanto prowls like a restless panther . . . and 14,000 fanatical Indonesians chant 'Kill! Kill! Kill!'

One of the great moments in sport! Even at our more modest standard, level doubles is an exciting all-action game, and one in which you will always enjoy participating.

Court formations

Basically two are used: the partners switching from one to the other in the course of a rally.

In **defence**, when you lift to the rear-court, you and your partner will each take up position near the centre of your service-court in a 'side-by-side' formation. Rackets outstretched to the side cover the width of the court. Two long strides forwards or backwards enable you to return drops or attacking clears.

In **attack**, you will take up a 'back and front' formation. When, in their turn, your opponents lift to your rear court, the nearest player obviously moves back to strike the shuttle. Even as he dances back, his partner darts into the T-junction to fill a gaping void and to be poised there, ready, racket raised, before his partner even hits it.

Thus, any weak return resulting from the 'back' player's smash can be attacked by the 'front' player before it drops below tape-height. This it would certainly have done had the smasher had to run in to retrieve it. The attack would have been lost – not sustained.

Once the attack is gained this formation is maintained as long as either player is hitting down or playing so tight to the net that their opponents are forced to lift again and again . . . In this context even a delicate net-shot or a drop-shot that forces a lift is an attacking shot. The net player must try to maintain the attack from the forecourt, his partner, from the rear court.

If either 'lifts' to the rear-court with lob or clear, they have lost the attack, and are on the defensive. And they must consequently revert to 'sides'. But which side? If the net-player lobs, he is presumably under pressure, so he drops quickly back to the *nearest* service-court. His partner can see this and equally quickly completes the defensive wall by moving into the other service-court.

If it is the rear court player who clears, the alert net player knows from his opponents' last shot – and the sound of his partner's

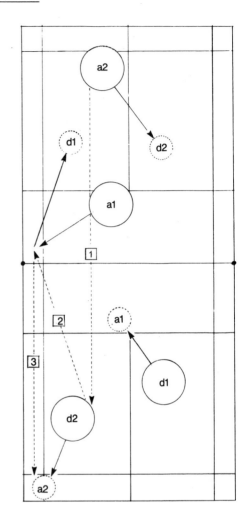

Changing position in men's and ladies' doubles. D1 and d2 move from defence to attack (a1 and a2) when a1 lobs d2's net shot and d2 intercepts; a1 and a2 move from attack to defence (d1 and d2).

feet – where the latter is. He moves swiftly into the other service-court.

In theory it sounds simple enough. In early practice, when smashes are not hit down, clears are short, and net-shots high, the net player has little time to think positionally. Hopefully, a safety reflex will send him scuttling back when faced with the prospect of a shuttle in the face from the upraised racket of a mid-court 'smasher' or 'net-dabber'. But with experience, and more accurate shots, the changes become as automatic as riding a bicycle! After all, both defence and attack positions are just simple common-sense, aren't they?

General tactics

The technique and general tactical aim of each stroke has already been described. Now only a rather more specific description is needed. Men's and ladies' doubles are played with basically the same tactics. But on account of ladies' comparatively weaker smashing and slower movement there are slight differences of approach which are dealt with at the end of this section.

At the outset both pairs take up back and front positions, each optimistic that they will gain the attack. Note how important is the server's partner's role. Crouched astride the centre line, he must be able to return 'rushes' into the body, spring forward to take half-court returns early; or backwards to intercept lobs. Almost as important is the receiver's partner, standing mid-court and to one side of the receiver. When the latter leaps forward to attack the serve, he must be ready to maintain that initiative at the back with smash, drop or shots to the net.

Serving

If points are to be won this is vitally important. The low serve to the T-junction area narrows your opponent's angle of return and, theoretically, gives you and your partner a better chance to intercept his return. If the receiver is lethal head-on, move your base a little to one side, though appreciating you've left a larger gap for a net return. Or serve to the side-line – though now, from the right court, you've made your partner's backhand vulnerable to attack and generally opened the angles. Always follow

Service target areas

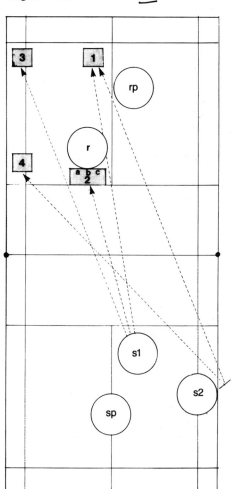

s1 = server's first option.
s2 = server's second option.
sp = server's partner.
r = receiver.
rp = receiver's partner.
1 = drive, flick or high.
2(a,b,c) = low (forehand, body, backhand).
3 = flick or high.
4 = low.

in thoughtfully on your low serve, watching your opponent's racket keenly, and looking for a net cut-off.

A well-disguised flick may temper your opponent's aggression. A flick to the centre runs the risk of falling into the wrong court. One to the side-line opens the angles but it does also drive the receiver from the centre, gives him a rather more difficult shot to play, and, with its extra distance, gives you the opportunity to flick more crisply, and therefore surprisingly, without overshooting the back service line. The drive should at least be tried tentatively to test a suspect backhand.

If nothing else is effective, a very high serve – or three, no more – may work by forcing mis-hits from a joyous and over-confident receiver who forgets that in receiving such a serve timing is more difficult and the shuttle dropping vertically is harder to hit cleanly. Even try an angled flat drive following in for a weak return to the net. With all these variants never overplay your hand – and do be ready for a quick reply. Use both forehand and backhand serves.

Return of serve

Your aim is to meet every serve early – *chest-high, in front of the service line.* So be fast and aggressive off a forward base. Don't, however, throw away a point by rushing into the net a shuttle that was above it when you moved but has fallen below it by the time you hit it.

Dab low serves steeply down into knees or gap if you can. If not, use a tight net-shot to the corner most distant from the server. An admirable compromise for returning the shuttle tape-high or just below, is the deceptive half-court push. It must be fast enough to beat the incoming server yet drop short of the thrusting back player. Avoid the

Return of serve target areas

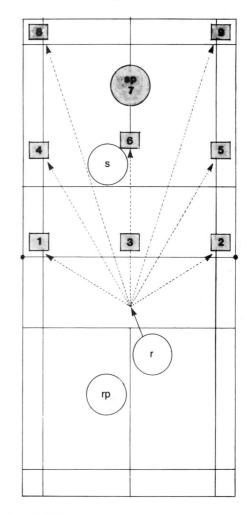

s = server.
sp = server's partner.
r = receiver.
rp = receiver's partner.
1,2,3 = target areas for net shots.
4,5,6 = target areas for half-court pushes.
7 = target area for fast rush to body.
8,9 = target areas for fast rushes to back 'boxes'.

The power of the follow through is shown here by China's Liu Jua but he will quickly regain his poise to counter the return.

lob like the plague! If you must lift, then do it early, fast, deep and not too high – to the *backhand*.

In returning high or flick serves smash straight, unless you are definitely attacking the weaker player, and steeply, into an inviting gap, down the middle, or into the defender's inner side. Drops should be played to the middle, to cause doubt, or to the slower or less consistent player. Clears off a flick should be high to give you time to recover, and straight if you feel better equipped than your partner to deal with the return. In this server-receiver battle the odds are stacked in your favour. Gain the attack . . . and keep it.

Attack

Rear Court This in mid-rally is the same as off a high serve. Anything short of the back service-line should be smashed – and smashed again. Just occasionally, an attacking clear may catch out too firmly rooted defenders. From between the back tram-lines, play drops to force another lift, a shorter lift . . .

At the net If rear-court attack is to be effectively backed up you must have your racket up and be on the balls of your feet. Yes, literally, for you have only a split second to make your interception. Watch your opponent's action and racket-head at impact to get an 'early warning' start. Strokes played are much as in return of low serve: the dab and the upward net-shot. If the latter is returned with another net-shot, don't be chicken, don't, in blind panic, lift. Keep it on the net – unless, of course, your opponent is altogether too good for you there.

Try not to be drawn right out to the sideline or you will be swiftly cross-courted. Reach for the line with foot and racket and you will still be placed to cut off a cross-court reply. Always be menacing, but take only what you can control effectively.

Defence

Was it Clausewitz, the great military strategist, who said, 'the best form of defence is attack'? I'm not sure, but I most certainly commend the maxim. Don't be a poor fish and stay wriggling on the hook!

By anticipation and agility meet drop-shots early enough to turn them into lift-forcing net-shots, or even to hit them down for a winner. If lob you must, then fast, to a *length* and to the backhand. Be prepared for the occasional flat attacking clear – spring back and attack with smash or drop. Push back dabs from the net flat with quick reflexed arm action *away* from the menacing net-player.

The smash is the big gun you *must* spike. If it is sluggish and flat, move in and push, or drive flat and fast into the smasher's body or witheringly cross-court. Or move in further still, to dab in crouch defence. If it is powerful, drop back to draw its sting a little – but beware of drops to the now exposed forecourt. You will have to lob but at least swing your opponent from side to side – it's tiring and error provoking. Try and ensure length.

Ladies' doubles variations

Low serves will be returned tight to the net more often than rushed and fast lobs to the backhand may be played more effectively and safely. Since defence invariably over-rides attack, smashes should be steeper, more accurately placed and played from less far back in court. Flat clears, especially to what may be a frail backhand, are useful alternatives. Drop-shots can be used more with less fear of fast interception.

Net play becomes even more important. Tight net-shots may force the necessary short lift or be winners in their own right. As the back player's smash will not normally be strong enough to summarily end rallies, quicksilver footwork and fast reflexes are essential to administer the *coup de grâce*. Remember, always keep alert!

MIXED · DOUBLES

Mixed hockey and mixed football are generally received by athletic men with a patronizing smirk as a pleasant romp, and by ladies with some trepidation but a fiercely determined 'I'll show them' approach.

Not so in badminton, Jill can be as big a threat as Jack – and score as many winners. She more than pays her corner. As a result mixed is a fascinating third game. With its accent on touch, deception, flatness of trajectory and new tactics, it is as different as chalk from cheese from the rougher, tougher hurly-burly of men's doubles.

Let us, however, be under no illusions. Few ladies, if any, are as fast or powerful in rear court as a man. If they played there, the opposing man would run them ragged. So a system of court coverage must be devised both to counter this and to capitalize on the ladies' strengths of swift reflex, neat movement, quickness of eye and delicacy of touch. In general terms, therefore, the lady plays, a little sheltered, 'at the net'; the man does the donkey-work 'at the back'.

The lady's role

The 'Great Male I Am' will doubtless beat his chest and boast 'I cover more than twice the court area than the lady does'. True. But what he so conveniently forgets is this:

1 The lady at the net has half the time to see the shuttle that is travelling twice as fast!

2 She is cramped, caught between an equally threatening female only a couple of yards away on the other side of a net she mustn't touch, and a heavy-breathing, thumping male just behind her.

3 And, unlike the cowardly male in men's doubles, there is no retreat from the net for her when a smash is threatened.

4 Moreover, she cannot see, only guess, what her partner is doing.

So, gentlemen, when your lady does make a mistake, do not, as is the way with too many men, roll your eyes beseechingly to heaven or drop your racket in feigned stupefaction – all with a resigned sigh that can be heard a mile away.

Let's deal with her first as an individual – although always remembering that for all the clear-cut guide-lines of court coverage mixed is a partnership. Each player seeks to make an opening for the other; each tries to avoid putting the other 'on the spot'.

Position   The lady covers across the court from side-line to side-line, and from net to front service-line. Until she can smash and defend like a man she will be 'on base' in this area throughout the game – except when driven back with a flick or high serve.

This at first is a daunting thought. A horrendous one when you first play there with shuttles buzzing past you like angry bees. A sheer delight when you have found your feet – and touch – and are making nonchalent winners off the increasingly frustrated men's best shots.

Your general base is on the T-junction of centre-line and front service-line. There you stand, no, bounce, on the balls of your feet, watching intently and intelligently your opponents' action to gain an early inkling of the shuttle's flight. Then with racket, in frying-pan grip probably, at tape-height, you dance or lunge in to meet it at the earliest possible moment.

Serving   The ability to serve really low to the centre, to 'narrow the angle', is a tremendous asset. It forces a lift to you or your partner, and puts you odds-on favourite to win the rally. If you serve to the centre, the shuttle, in theory at least, will generally be returned within your's or your partner's reach. If you serve to the side-line, away from a menacing male racket, you make life difficult by 'opening the angles', i.e. by giving your opponent a chance to hit straight – or, suddenly, cross-court. If you serve thus from the right court you give your opponent a clear invitation to attack your partner's perhaps frail backhand. From the left court, it is less dangerous.

As long as you are 'getting the lift', serve low. Your partner can't ask for more. As very occasional variants, try a probing drive to the backhand or a flick to the slower moving lady. Do not serve these any more than absolutely necessary to the faster-reacting man. As your partner has the whole width of a deep court to cover, it is not a good way to gain his approval. If you adopt 'crouch defence' you'll find it best to serve 'flicks' to the outside corners. And whether it is drive or flick be prepared for a very smart reply. Serve from as near the front service line as possible so that you can take net returns early, or simply give a realistic impression of a shuttle-hungry tigress and so force a lift to your grateful partner.

Returning serve If you can also return service well (i.e. downwards) you are a pearl beyond price who will never lack partners. You simply must be aggressive, able to accelerate away from your alert position of readiness so that you can attack low serve and flick alike. A tall order. One to be practised and practised. Bad low serves you will dab down steeply at the floor or into your opponent's body. Beware above all things of (1) the *flat* dab that screams out of the back of the court like a hedge-hopping Harrier jet and, (2) the death-wish, rising push straight onto your opponent's racket, instead of into a gap or the body.

If you are not quite quick enough to hit *down,* a deceptive half-court push between man and lady, to what, for married couples unwise enough to play together, is known as 'the divorce area', is invaluable. If you really must lift, then a tight upward net return away from the server, not cross-court straight onto the oncoming server's racket, is the answer. Don't – please DON'T, aimlessly, like a petrified rabbit, just hoist the shuttle to your unbelieving male opponent to hammer through you – and the floor. A quick, flattish, deceptive lift to the backhand is permissible

– on rare occasions.

When your partner receives, you will stand in front of him, just to left or right. Later, when you have developed a worthwhile smash, he will ask you to stand a little to one side and behind him to cover the back of the court, if he is stranded at the net or needs to stay there to finish off the rally. When your partner serves there is a change. You stay in the left-hand court whichever side he serves from. This makes a reply to your forehand more likely.

Returning the flick serve effectively is vastly more difficult. Having bounced back to hit it you then have in virtually the same action to power your way back to the net. The man must stay at the back but if it is a match – and he is a gentleman – he will help out, reluctantly, by taking returns to the most distant third of the net.

You simply must not show the white feather by clearing. If you do, you will quickly meet the shuttle again – as a sitting or at least a slow-moving duck. Show this is all you can do and the man will relentlessly serve deep to elicit a weak reply and you will become a battered target.

If you are on balance and have an accurate fast smash go for a gap and try and force a return to your side of the court. If not, a steep fast drop-shot to half-court will cause some dissention between your opponents, force a lift, and give you more time to recover.

Serve and return are 60 per cent of the lady's game. Think them out and *practise* them!

Attack This is very similar to returning serve. All depends on your positioning, speed of foot and eye, and therefore ability to meet the shuttle early. Move a little to the side your partner is attacking so that you can step in to a cramped return. If he is

Zhao Jianua of China is off the ground as he smashes down the line

stranded at one side of the court, or has smashed too straight and flat down the line so giving your opponent his eagerly sought chance to attack, move a little the other way, cross-court. Quick thinking is needed.

Shots below the tape return with tight net shots to the corners. Keep it there – show who's mistress. With your opponent lured off balance or too near the post play a cross-court shot, flat, fast to the opposite side-line.

Those taken fractionally above tape-level can be best dealt with by the invaluable half-court shot. It draws the man in and pushes the lady back, forces a lift . . . Above? Then, of course, the *steep* rally-winning dab to body or into a gap.

Defence Your duties here will depend on your abilities – and consultation with your partner. If your defence is weak he will leave you to crouch at the net while he shoulders the entire burden. If your eye is good he will ask you to drop back behind the front service-line to return a cross-court smash with the crouch defence shot (This leaves your opposite front corner vulnerable, so decide with your partner who takes the drop there.) With minimal backswing try and dab down into or away from the smasher. Only when you can cope with a man's smash – *and* be able to counter his alternative attacking clear with a lusty smash – will your partner ask you to drop back to 'sides' as in level doubles.

Combining Finally, remember you are a pair. Try to elicit lifted shots that his heaviest artillery can attack. Equally, avoid lifting and so leaving him desperately covering the whole court.

Have a clear understanding with your partner which shots you each take. If you can intercept half-court shots he will be delighted. But deciding what to take and what to leave can be as difficult as playing a shot. Never drop back far behind the front service-line – he gets rather touchy at having, what for him, advancing, is an easy

Mixed doubles attack against crouch defence

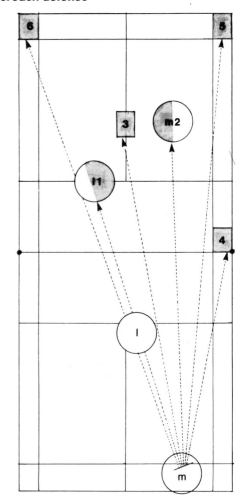

l = *lady.*
m = *man.*
1 = *smash at lady.*
2 = *smash at man's right side.*
3 = *smash between the two.*
4 = *straight drop.*
5,6 = attacking *clears.*

winner, taken off his racket in a face to face encounter with an off-balance partner mid-court. Nor, perversely, is he pleased if you start to intercept – then stop and suddenly leave it all to him. Take only those shots – generally just in front of your ears – that you can *effectively control*. Not too much – and not too little! Oh, and don't forget the Nora Perry smile and consoling bottom-tap for an erring partner.

The man's role

You have of course not skipped 'The Lady's Role' but read it as slowly and thoughtfully as she did. So you now have a better idea of what the, sometimes, unpredictable sex is going to do. She too will read this so that she knows what the unseen, gallumphing creature behind her is up to.

Position A position of readiness astride the centre-line, or, if your backhand is a touch frail, a *little* to that side. Very much on the balls of your feet for you have a large area to cover. Very much too, eye on the shuttle. Do not hug the back of the court or there will be a gap in front of you; equally don't crowd in on your partner, charming though she may be, or there is an even nastier gap behind you. Let's settle for 'equidistant' – an excellent word to bear in mind.

Serving As, unlike in men's, you have no partner behind you, you must serve from deeper in court, say 1·5–1·8m (5–6ft) behind the front service line. Have your partner always in front to your left and as near the centre line as she can by leaning to the left to avoid baulking your opponents. Yes, this certainly gives your opponents longer to see the shuttle but the opposing man, with no one behind him, is also more chary of rushing in, with open court behind him.

'Low to the man', 'high to the lady' is no bad maxim at this stage – provided the lady does not pack a punch. If she does, it's low to both, to the centre, with a flick as an occasional mixer. A drive down the lady's backhand is a good idea – an angled drive still better provided you and your partner know precisely who takes the block to the net or the clear to the back. If played flat it can be morale shaking.

Returning serve Here the pattern is much the same as in men's – with two provisos. (1) Remember you have no one behind you so if a winner is not 'on', play a return, often half-court, that will give you time to regain base; (2) be less aggressive on the man's serve – and more aggressive on the lady's.

In the latter case, take a chance with your first return. If you can crunch it with a return straight at the face or the body you *may* well shake her morale. And by shaking her serving, you may shake her net-play also.

Attack Understand first that neither you nor your opponents are going to lift unless forced to. Therefore much of the game is played flat, from mid-court, down the side-lines.

A fairly regular pattern emerges. A half-court return of serve to your forehand (or backhand). Take it high but probably below tape-level so your return is a deceptive half-court push. Your opponent, in the same boat, counters with the same move again. So do you. And so does he.

This probing for an opening goes on until the opposing lady decides to chip in with a winner; or perhaps a half-hit return that you can hit cross-court to the far corner of the net – or at her. (Cast gentlemanliness to the winds and remember, if the opposing man is strong, play on what may be the much weaker lady. Have no qualms about it!)

If the lady does not intervene, you wait for a male push that is too high, too deep. Now you attack. Not with a smash, the shuttle is not high enough for that. But with a flat, fast drive straight down the side-line into the 'box', or, across court, to the opposite tram-lines.

Your opponent will counter, if he is quick,

with another drive, straight or cross-court; if he is only fairly quick then it's back to the half-court probing; if he is slow he may have to resort to a net-shot to your lady or a lift to your backhand which you will endeavour to kill round-the-head.

Beware of 'cross-courtitis'. It is infectious, exhilarating, but entirely predictable. If you play cross-court every time, as many club players do, your opponent knows what is coming. So use it sparingly only when (1) you can hit flat or down, and, (2) when your steady drip of straight, deceptive half-court pushes has brought both your opponents to one side, and thus cleared the centre of the court.

On occasions the shuttle will be lifted. If the lift is short, smash – to the side-lines, or to the body to force a return to your eager partner. If the lady adopts crouch defence then smash *steeply* at her. Hit flat – and she may have it on the floor before you can blink. If it is deep, then a *fast* drop-shot (with a lady ready at the net, the slow drop is suicide). Again to the invaluable half-court No Man's Land. Another form of attack, if you think the opposing lady is slow, is to try and run her to and fro across-court with accurate flat net-shots.

Defence Here with two-thirds of the court to cover, you have problems – the reasons why neither man nor woman willingly lifts. Try and see the length of lob or clear – by looking at your opponent's feet. If it is really

deep expect a fast drop – return it with push or net-shot. If it is short, cover the side to which the more likely straight smash will go. What now? If it's flat, push or drive it straight or cross-court according to your opponent's position.

Should it be the lady attacking you from the net with dabs to the body, be on your toes to side-step if you can. If not then it must be quick reflexed, straight-armed pushes through her, or at her, or net-shots to the corners.

Try always quickly to regain the attack with shrewd placements and a never-say-die determination. Remember how difficult is your partner's task. So play to set up winners for her; encourage and, if need be, console her and always consult her. A friendly post-mortem after a game will help both of you to know which of your shots helps your partner, and which puts her in deep trouble.

England's Julie Bradbury readies forward for a shot at the net in an All-England Championship Match in 1992.

USEFUL ADDRESSES

Australian Badminton Association
PO Box 629
Kew 3101
Victoria

Bangladesh Badminton Federation
Stadium
Dacca 2
Bangladesh

Canadian Badminton Association
1600 James Naismith Drive
Gloucester
Ontario
Canada K1B 5NL

Badminton Association of England
National Badminton Centre
Bradwell Road
Loughton Lodge
Milton Keynes
MK8 9LA

The Badminton Umpires Association of England
c/o National Badminton Centre
Bradwell Road
Loughton Lodge
Milton Keynes MK8 9LA

English Schools Badminton Association
National Badminton Centre
Bradwell Road
Loughton Lodge
Milton Keynes MK8 9LA

Badminton Association of India
Jackson's Hotel
Jabalpur (MP) 482001
India

The International Badminton Federation
24 Winchcombe House
Winchcombe Street
Cheltenham
Gloucestershire GL52 2NA

The Badminton Union of Ireland
The House of Sport
Upper Malone Road
Belfast BT9 5LA
Northern Ireland

Jamaica Badminton Association
PO Box 264
Kingston 6
Jamaica

Kenya Badminton Association
PO Box 40142
Nairobi
Kenya

BADMINTON

The Badminton Association of Malaysia
Kuala Lumpar Badminton Stadium
3½ Miles Jalan Cheras
56000
Kuala Lumpur
Malaysia

Badminton Association of Malta
PO Box No 599
Valletta
Malta

New Zealand Badminton Federation
PO Box 11-319
Wellington
New Zealand

Amateur Badminton Association of Nigeria
National Sports Commission
National Stadium
Box 145
Surulere
Lagos
Nigeria

Pakistan Badminton Federation
297-A(11)
New Muslim Town
Lahore
Pakistan

Scottish Badminton Union
Cockburn Centre
40 Bogmoor Place
Glasgow G51 4TQ
Scotland

South African Badminton Union
PO Box 26154
Arcadia
Pretoria 0007
Republic of South Africa

United States Badminton Association
902 'O' Street
Lincoln
Nebraska 68508
USA

Welsh Badminton Union
3rd floor
3 Westgate Street
Cardiff
Wales CF1 1DD

RULES CLINIC

INDEX

INDEX